KNOCKOUT

Short Stories

Selected and edited
by Jane Joyner

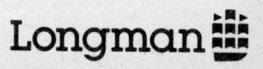

Longman

LONGMAN GROUP UK LIMITED,
Longman House, Burnt Mill, Harlow,
Essex CM20 2JE, England
and Associated Companies throughout the world.

Editorial material © Longman Group UK Limited 1988
Stories © Robert Leeson Jan Mark Jenny Hursell Michael
Rosen Adèle Geras Terry Deary David Rees Beverley Naidoo
1988

All rights reserved; no part of this publication
may be reproduced, stored in a retrieval system,
or transmitted in any form or by any means, electronic,
mechanical, photocopying, recording, or otherwise,
without the prior written permission of the Publishers
or a licence permitting restricted copying issued by the Copyright
Licensing Agency Ltd, 33–34 Alfred Place, London, WC1E 7DP.

First published 1988
Second impression 1990

Set in 11½/15point Cheltenham
Produced by Longman Group Far East Ltd.
Printed in Hong Kong

ISBN 0 582 24393 9

Contents

	page
Introduction	iv
Never Kiss Frogs! *Robert Leeson*	1
Do You Read Me? *Jan Mark*	21
Statements of Account *Jenny Hursell*	35
Maureen *Michael Rosen*	49
The Centre *Adèle Geras*	65
The Consett Giants *Terry Deary*	89
Cliff *David Rees*	109
The Typewriter *Beverley Naidoo*	127

Introduction

These stories have been chosen to appeal to most teenagers. There should be something here for almost everyone. Don't feel you have to begin with the first story and read through to the last one. Dip in and out of the book. Read the short introduction to each story to see which one is likely to be your favourite. If you've enjoyed another Knockout by one of these authors you may decide to go straight to that author's story. Perhaps you will be drawn to a story by its title alone.

Once you've read the story don't feel you have to do anything else. Most people read for pleasure, not so they can do some writing about what they've read.

If you want to do some writing about a story, or if you have to for a coursework folder, you will find two suggestions for writing at the end of each story. These suggestions are designed to produce substantial pieces of work which will be the result of reading, thinking, discussing, note-making, drafting and redrafting. Some of the suggestions could take you as long as a week to write properly. If you have a better idea

INTRODUCTION

for a piece of writing than the ones suggested here do that after discussing your idea with someone else.

Happy reading!

Never Kiss Frogs

Robert Leeson

Robert Leeson was born in Cheshire. He gained a scholarship to grammar school and began work on the local newspaper at the age of sixteen. He then joined the army and, after several jobs, he returned to journalism. He began to write children's stories in the 1960s, trying them out on his own children first. Robert Leeson likes to visit schools to help young people with their own writing and to find out what they think of his books. Pupils proved essential when he was writing his four *Grange Hill* books.

Other Knockouts by Robert Leeson are *Time Rope*, *Three Against the World*, *At War with Tomorrow* and *The Metro Gangs Attack* (a serial novel in four books).

Never Kiss Frogs!

This is a modern version of a traditional fairy story with many of the elements changed. The prince is not charming and the princess is a working class, strong-minded teenager who learns that kissing frogs is not a very good idea.

Never Kiss Frogs!

Gail was a nice girl. Sometimes she behaved well. Sometimes she behaved badly. Sometimes she worked hard. Sometimes she was idle. Sometimes she got on with her friends. Sometimes she had a row with them. She was just about average, was Gail.

But there was one thing different about her.

She had one funny habit.

Gail kissed frogs.

Well, she tried. It's not all that easy. It seems easy enough. They sit there very quiet under a stone or a leaf. Thet don't move. They don't even blink when you look at them. And their lips stick out a bit, as though they're waiting for someone to give them a big smacking kiss.

But you try and do it.

For one thing. You have to get your face down two inches off the ground. It's very awkward, but that's the way frogs are made. Well, you wouldn't fancy it if they were six foot high, would you?

The trouble is, once you've got down on your knees, then crouched down a bit further, and just when you've got your face nice and close to those great, big beady, fascinating eyes, just when you're ready to plonk one on him – or her – what do they do?

Well, you know, don't you? They jump. They jump about three feet. Now you may not think three feet is much of a jump. Daley Thompson could do a lot better. But it's a long way for a frog. And it doesn't half put you off when you're trying to kiss one.

Which is probably why not many people do it?

But Gail did.

And why? I hear you asking. Well, I'm going to tell you.

She had two reasons.

The first was she didn't like kissing boys.

Why not? What's wrong with boys?

Well, for a start, they're sticky, they don't wash behind their ears and to be honest, they pong a bit ... Do you want me to go on?

What about girls? then, I can hear you saying. If you think they all smell like roses, you're mistaken.

Well, the fact was – Gail didn't like kissing boys.

But there was another reason. She'd read in a book somewhere that when a girl kissed a frog, he turned into a prince. Not like Prince Charles (he's married anyway) or Prince Andrew (so's he), but a prince with a castle and about two thousand bags of gold and a father who's just about to pop off and leave his kingdom. There's a big wedding, because the prince is grateful and wants to reward the girl who kissed him, and they all live happily ever after.

And Gail was quite keen on living happily ever after. There were times when she was fed up with life. She lived at home with her mother. Her Dad wasn't around, and her mother had to work to keep them both. And to make a proper living, they took in lodgers. So Gail and her mother lived in the basement. The lodgers lived upstairs. And there was a lot of cooking and washing and cleaning. It went on most evenings and every weekend.

Sometimes Gail helped her mother. Sometimes she didn't feel like it. So her mother would just shrug her shoulders and go on working. Then Gail would feel awful and go and help her.

So every now and then Gail would wish that just for once they could have a house all to themselves and enough money not to have to be frying bacon and sausage, and washing up, and taking loads down to the launderette for other people.

Sometimes, when she was fed up Gail would go out in the garden at the back. It was a sort of garden. Every now and then her Mum would go berserk with spades and forks and rakes. Then she'd give up and the grass would grow and the weeds would sprout and the flower beds would disappear and the place would look like Tarzan's back yard.

It wasn't so bad when the sun was shining and the birds were singing. But when it rained, the leaves dripped and the grass was sopping wet and the place ponged a bit where the cats had been. It wasn't all that marvellous at all.

One day, Gail had a row with her mother. She went out into the garden for a sulk. There'd been a shower and the sun had just come out again. Everything was damp and steamy. And as Gail got to the bottom of the garden, and was standing there looking for something to kick, she suddenly realised that someone was looking at her. She looked round – there was no one there. No one in the garden. No one over the hedge next door. No one in the windows. She was alone. But she wasn't. She knew she was being watched.

Then she saw it, sitting under a dock leaf, big beady eyes staring, breathing in and out, the biggest, fattest, grottiest looking frog. For a moment or two they looked at each other, then the frog spoke.

'Sweet lady. Please have pity on me.'

'You what?' said Gail. She didn't mean to be rude. Her mother was always trying to get her to say 'Beg pardon' or something like that. But it just came out.

'Have pity on a poor creature in distress,' said the frog.

Gail crouched down and very carefully put her face a few inches from the frog's. The frog didn't move. Didn't even draw itself together like they do before they take off.

'My story,' said the frog, 'is a long and sad one . . . '

But Gail couldn't wait. She knew what she had to do. She squeezed up her mouth and gave the frog a great big smacker of a kiss right in the middle of his sentence.

There was a sudden noise. It wasn't like a trumpet blast, or a cannon going off. It was more like the sound of a blown-up paper bag bursting. Then Gail found herself staring, not at the frog any more, but at a pair of highly polished leather boots. She sat back in surprise, then jumped up again as the wet from the grass soaked through her knickers.

Standing in front of her was a tall, handsome

man, with wavy blonde hair and sky blue eyes, dressed in the most stunning red and gold uniform. He was like a living box without the chocolates.

'Oh, great,' breathed Gail. 'A real prince. Smashing.'

She spread out her skirt, went down on one knee and said. 'Your humble servant, your Highness.'

The Prince looked down at her, raised his eyebrows and said:

'Oh, blow.'

'You wha- I mean, I beg your pardon, your gracious ...'

'I mean,' said the Prince. 'You're a bit younger than I expected ...'

'I'm nearly eleven,' retorted Gail, a little more sharply than she meant to. 'I'm starting at Hob Lane Comprehensive this autumn.'

'Comprehensive?' The Prince looked baffled. Gail didn't try to explain. She guessed he'd never been to a comprehensive anyway. She was a bit put out, now.

'What's wrong with me? I kissed you didn't I? I rescued you from the wicked enchantress didn't I? I broke the spell. What more did you want?'

He drew himself up a little further. His chest

inside the red jacket swelled up.

'There is no need to be impertinent. I am, of course, grateful for your help. But according to the rules I am supposed to marry you. And to be quite frank, you are under age.'

'Gail!' Mum was calling from the basement window. 'Will you come in? It's going to start raining any minute.'

'Won't be a minute, Mum,' Gail shouted back. She was thinking fast. This wasn't turning out as she expected. It'd be another five years at least before she could marry the Prince. And how was she going to keep him hanging about? She played for time.

'Your Highness. My name is Gail.' She waved a hand. 'This is our humble abode. Would you care to partake of . . . ' – she tried to think what they were having for supper and what the posh name for it was. Fishburgers – oh no.

'You, Gail!' Gail nearly jumped out of her skin. Her mother was standing right by her. For a moment she thought the Prince was going to be invisible. But no such luck.

'Who's this? And what's he doing in fancy dress? Is he looking for a room? The top one's empty.'

At the sound of her voice, the Prince turned round and looked straight at Gail's mother. She went red. She blushed and started patting her hair. Then she fiddled with the apron she had on over her shirt and trousers.

Oh no, thought Gail, this is getting complicated.

'Er, Prince – I'm afraid I don't know your name. This is my mother.'

'Prince Rupert,' answered the man in red. 'But, surely not your mother. Perhaps your sister?'

Oh, he's one of those, thought Gail. Then she looked at her mother again. What was up with her? She was going all soppy.

'I'm Jackie, short for Jacqueline,' said Mum, her voice going squeaky with embarrassment.

'Would you like to come in for a cup of tea?' Mum pulled herself together and started taking charge. They walked towards the back door and Gail trailed along behind. This was not turning out right at all.

Things got worse. Prince Rupert had a very hearty appetite. He ate six fishburgers (there were only eight in the packet), drank seven cups of tea. There was hardly anything left for Gail and her mum. Gail noticed, but her mum didn't seem to.

Prince Rupert chatted on about his life at court, how big the castle was, how many carriages there were, how many servants, how old his father was – just about ready to retire. He went on all about how happy his life had been until the terrible day when a wicked witch had taken a dislike to the family and put a spell on him. And ever since he'd been living in this damp hole in the ground.

Huh, thought Gail, this basement isn't much better. The point was how soon could they move into the castle? that's what she wanted to know. But every time she wanted to ask an important question like that, her mum said: 'Please don't keep interrupting, Gail. I've told you about that before, you talk far too much. You were saying, Prince Rupert?'

And Prince Rupert didn't even seem to notice her getting told off. He seemed to have forgotten completely which fair maiden had rescued him.

In fact, thought Gail, she was beginning to go off him. Now she looked at him, she realised that Simon Robinson, who was doorman at the Bingo Club, looked just as smart in his uniform and he did listen when you spoke to him.

Suddenly it struck her. She knew what was going to happen. Mum was going to marry Prince Rupert, and she was going to be a Prince's step-daughter. That wasn't so good.

Gail knew what happened to step-daughters in fairy tales. It was about time she sorted things out.

'I say,' she burst out. 'I say' is the posh way you interrupt people. 'I say.'

They both stopped talking and looked at her.

'Where is this castle of yours?'

'Why just a half mile away,' answered Prince Rupert. 'I was hunting in the forests beyond the castle walls when the wicked witch turned me into a frog.'

'Well, there's no castle for miles round here,' declared Gail.

'Don't be so rude, our Gail,' said her mother. But Prince Rupert looked baffled.

'Perhaps,' he said loftily, 'the wicked witch has enchanted the castle away.'

Just my flaming luck, thought Gail. But she wasn't giving up yet.

'What's your father's kingdom called, then?'

Her mother tried to stare Gail down, but she repeated her question.

'Muscovia,' replied Prince Rupert.

'Where's that?'

'Why, all around as far as a man can ride in seven days and seven nights.'

'You're joking. This is Westchester,' retorted

Gail, 'and we ought to know. We've lived here all our lives.'

Prince Rupert went red in the face.

'How dare you contradict me? Impudent vixen.' He stood up. 'I shall not stay here a moment longer, in this hovel. I shall return to the castle immediately.'

Mum jumped up and grabbed the prince by the arm.

'Now, please, your Highness, do calm down. I'm sure no offence was meant. Please stay the night. I have a room empty.'

'There's only the box room,' said Gail. She was really putting the boot in now.

'No there's not,' snapped her mother. 'The others can all move up one and he can have the best room.'

Prince Rupert sat down. 'Very well. I will stay the night. And out of gratitude, I shall forget the insult. I shall not even ask that your daughter be soundly thrashed, although that is what she deserves.'

Gail was ready to explode. But her mother was already out of the room getting things sorted out. The lodgers didn't like it, but before they knew where they were, they were all shifted up one room and Prince Rupert was fixed up in the best room. Mum even found an old pair of pyjamas from the chest of drawers for him.

So Prince Rupert stayed the night, and the next night and the next. He didn't even go out. In fact he stayed in bed until afternoon most days and then he would get up for supper, eat a lot, drink some wine or a bottle of Guinness Mum brought from the off-license, talk a lot about life at court and go to bed again. The lodgers thought it was a bit of a giggle at first, but in the end they got fed up of hearing his stories and went off down the pub.

And they got even more fed up because Mum was so busy seeing to Prince Rupert, that she didn't bother about cooking their meals properly or cleaning the house – apart from the best room.

What was worse, when Gail went to school, she found no one really believed her when she said she'd kissed a frog and it turned into a prince. In fact they even made rude remarks about it. When Gail told the whole story during a story-writing lesson, her teacher thought it was a very well written fantasy, but it would have been better if Gail didn't exaggerate quite so much.

Gail marched home that night and got out the encyclopedia from the cupboard. It had a

NEVER KISS FROGS!

big map of the world inside. She marched into the kitchen where Mum and Prince Rupert were having supper.

Opening the map out on the table she said:

'Now you show us where this Muscovia is.'

Mum looked really shocked, but Prince Rupert simply made a grand wave of his arm and then put his finger down right in the middle of Russia.

'There,' he said, 'the great kingdom of Muscovia.'

Next day, Gail told teacher. But teacher said. 'I think there's some mistake Gail. They don't have princes in Russia.'

Next week, the other lodgers moved out. They'd had enough of hearing Prince Rupert telling them: 'So, I said to the Grand Duke . . .'

But things got worse. Mum was so busy looking after Prince Rupert – and he needed an awful lot of looking after, with his uniform having to be laundered and ironed every day and his boots polished, and his breakfast and lunch served in bed. In the end she was later and later for work until she got the sack. But she didn't seem to notice.

The rest of the house got emptier and dustier. The weeds and grass in the garden grew like triffids. Prince Rupert lay in bed and called for his breakfast and his supper and his polished boots, and Mum ran to and fro whenever he called.

She began to look so pale and thin that Gail stopped feeling furious with her and began to feel worried. After a few weeks, Mum suddenly got the flu and had to stop in bed. She didn't really want to, but Gail made her.

She stopped off school to look after things. But after two days of Prince Rupert and his 'Bring me this, bring me that,' she'd had enough. That evening, when Mum was tucked up in bed and Prince Rupert was sitting noshing fried chicken in the best room, Gail got on the phone and spoke to Aunt Mandy. Aunt Mandy was tall and slim like Mum, but just a bit different in her ways. She drove a van for the local council and when she cornered, the old folk would say – here comes meals on two wheels.

She arrived next day, early and went through the house like a dose of salts. She marched into the best room. Gail closed her ears but she could still hear the banging and shouting. Then Aunt Mandy came out with that lovely red uniform under her arm.

'Right, Gail, stuff that lot in the boiler will you.'

NEVER KISS FROGS!

Suddenly Prince Rupert appeared in the doorway, in his underpants. He looked truly ridiculous.

'Where is my uniform, woman?' he demanded.

'Just going up in smoke, your worship,' answered Aunt Mandy.

'Here.'

From out of her bag she pulled a pair of jeans and an old shirt.

'Now get these on and get out in that garden and start cutting that grass.'

Prince Rupert went the colour of his trousers.

'How dare you, you impudent witch.'

Aunt Mandy took two steps towards him.

'Do you think I'm a witch?' she said, grinning a wicked grin.

Prince Rupert's face turned the colour of his underpants.

Without another word he took the shirt and jeans. He marched off to his room.

'I shall certainly not cut the grass. Get a gardener,' he said.

Aunt Mandy put her hands on her hips.

'No grass, no grub – mate,' she said.

Prince Rupert stuck it out until supper time. But next day when Gail came home from school, the garden was cleared, all the weeds were pulled up. It hadn't looked so good for years. Inside the kitchen Aunt Mandy and Prince Rupert were having a cup of tea. He had a bandage on his hand. Gail felt quite sorry for him.

'Oh did you cut your hand on the shears?' she asked.

'No, love, he burnt it making a cup of tea. But he's shaping up,' said Aunt Mandy.

So, it all turned out not too badly after all. Mum got better. She got her job back. And Prince Rupert got a part time job at the Bingo Club. When he called out 'All the sevens' in that posh voice of his, the old ladies loved it.

They didn't earn much, but it was enough for the three of them. And they didn't bother with lodgers any more. So Gail was able to live in the whole house after all. She quite got to like Rupert in the end – though not as much as her Mum did.

So they all lived happily ever after.

One day, after it had been raining, Gail was out in the garden pulling up weeds in the flower bed. And as she bent down, she had the feeling someone was watching her. You know that feeling you have.

And there under the azalea sat the biggest,

fattest grottiest looking frog you ever saw, gazing at her with his great, beady, fascinating eyes.

Then he spoke.

'Sweet lady. Have pity on me.'

Gail looked him straight in the eye.

'Listen buster. You have one minute to get out of here.'

Some ideas for writing

* Take another well-known fairy story or a traditional tale from any country and write your own modern version of it. You could change characters and part of the plot, like Robert Leeson has, as well as bringing the language up-to-date.

* Write a detailed account of exactly how Robert Leeson changes the traditional fairy story ideas in *Never Kiss Frogs!*. A good way to start would be to list all the things that people say and do in this story that they would never say and do in a proper fairy story. List things about the language that surprise you, look closely at the words people use. Next, in rough, write a paragraph explaining the change in each item on your list. Redraft your rough draft by fitting the paragraphs together in a sensible order and making sure you've said all you want to say without repeating yourself. Add a paragraph which concludes your essay by making it clear what you think the overall effect of these changes are. Now write your final draft.

DO YOU READ ME?

Jan Mark

Jan Mark was born in Hertfordshire and she grew up in North London and Kent. She taught art and English for six years and then left teaching to bring up a family. She wrote her first novel for children as a competition entry after her second baby was born. The novel won the competition and Jan Mark has written a great deal for young people since then, writing for radio and television as well as novels and short stories.

Jan Mark's other Knockout is *At the sign of the Dog and Rocket*.

Do You Read Me?

On the surface this looks like a typical school story but really it is more about communication than school. The language of the story is sophisticated and much of the humour is quite subtle. The ending of the story is left open and what happens next will depend on what kind of person you think Rodney is from the evidence in the story.

Do You Read Me?

It was the custom to bring back yearly reports, signed, at the beginning of the autumn term, to prove that they had been shown to parents, or at least to a competent forger. Fenton, the Fifth Year tutor, was at home in his office on Friday morning, to receive them. When Rodney King clinked in with his report and laid it on the desk under Fenton's nose, Fenton looked at it, looked at Rodney, crossed his knees, folded his hands, and sat back with the air of a man who has prepared a little speech.

'It's a good one, in most respects, especially for Art and Design, I see. A+, eh? Parents pleased?'

Rodney nodded.

'Only there's this nasty little rider here, to the effect that you have difficulty in communicating. What does that mean, do you think?'

Rodney shrugged.

'It could mean that you don't say much for yourself. Might that be the trouble? A bit of a loner, are you? No close friends?'

Rodney made a non-committal noise through the slit between his front teeth.

'Your written work's excellent – no complaints from anyone about that – but you've got to learn to verbalise. You'll be doing GCSE English, this year. What's going to happen when you come to the oral?'

Rodney's hand described a gesture that dealt dismissively with the English oral. He took a step backward to indicate that he thought the interview might usefully be concluded.

'It's no good relying on badges to do your communicating for you,' Fenton said. 'I mean, it's very reassuring to see you covered in slogans for Nuclear Disarmament and Rock against Racism, but any idiot can pin on a badge. How many have you got?'

Rodney was moved to verbalise. 'Seventy-three.'

'And are you wearing them all?'

'Yes, Sir.'

'Look, King, don't feel that I'm criticising gratuitously, but when the Headmaster abolished school uniform for the Fifth and Sixth Forms, I doubt if he intended you to come to school in armour plate. You look like a pearly king under a microscope. The people who sit behind you don't do any work; they spend all their time reading your badges.'

'I could move to the back,' Rodney offered, helpfully.

'Don't think of it,' Fenton said. 'We might lose touch with you altogether. Just move the badges from the rear of that cut-price Biggles outfit – and the sleeves. Be selective, King. Use your designer's eye. Just a few, here and there, tastefully arranged, should be quite aesthetically pleasing. We'll get the message – *one* message at a time. OK?'

Rodney returned to school on Monday with his bomber jacket feeling several pounds lighter, and ran into Fenton in the corridor where he was pinning a sheet of foolscap to the Fifth Year notice board.

'Book Fair,' said Fenton. 'October 8th, St Stephen's Hall. Want to come? Sign here.'

Rodney wove a deprecating pattern with his toes on the vinyl tiles, and the collar of his jacket rose about his ears.

'Oh, King, what eloquent shoulders you do have,' Fenton said. 'I'll take silence for consent. There, you can put your name down right at the top of the list. I suppose that elaborate routine is meant to suggest that you have nothing to write with? Tough titty,' said Fenton, whipping out his biro, and wrote Rodney's name in cockeyed capitals at the head of the paper. 'No one,' Fenton observed, 'would know that you hadn't written it yourself. And now I'll tell you something you'll really like. At this book fair they will have real live authors – and a badge-making machine.'

The lower forms went down to the Book Fair in supervised groups. The Fifth Year, as befitted the enormous strides that they had made in self-discipline during the summer holidays, were left to find their own way. Rodney attached himself wordlessly to a sauntering cluster comprising the visual cream of his class; Eddie Hobson, known as Hobbers, and his three followers; Anna Miles, Katy Matthews, and Liz Salkey, the one, by popular repute, promised to horrible Hobbers. Rodney suspected that they considered themselves too pretty to be seen associating with his own plain person, but knowing that if they told him to go away he would neither answer nor go away, they allowed him to slouch behind them to the hall.

Inside, they looked round in disdain.

'It's all kids' stuff,' Katy said. 'Little baby books and posters. Fenton's pulled a fast one on us.'

'All this way and nothing to read,' mourned

Hobbers, who had never yet been caught in possession of a book. 'Can't even read old King these days, since Fenton debadged him. I bet you took the filthy ones off, King.'

'He never had any filthy ones,' Anna said.

'He did,' said Hobbers, quietly, 'only he's so thick he didn't know they were filthy.' Liz, lovely Liz, said nothing at all.

Rodney set off round the hall. There were five live authors, all looking repellently like teachers, several thousand books, a man flogging literary T-shirts, and the badge-making machine. The queue for badges stretched down one side of the hall, and Rodney attached himself to the tail of it, feeling like Gulliver in Lilliput among so many first school children, all squeaking like unoiled roller skates. Fenton had reminded everyone to bring money with which to buy books, to be signed by the live authors. Rodney had brought two pounds with which he bought ten badge blanks. The little kids all round him were scrawling their names in orange or turquoise, and drawing Dracula, with bats. Rodney brought his A+ for Art and Design into play. Behind him he heard Liz addressing Hobbers.

'Let's each get a badge made. I'll have your name and you have mine.'

'Get out of it,' said the gallant Hobbers. 'I might get taken for King in a bad light.'

'I'll make you a badge, Liz,' Rodney said, suddenly, before he had time to lose courage. 'What would you like?'

'You stick to scribbling on your own walls, beautiful,' Hobbers said obscurely, with throaty threatening noises, and Liz was hauled away, badgeless.

Monday lunchtime brought Fenton and Rodney together again.

'I fear we're going to see a lot of each other this term,' Fenton sighed. 'You're sailing perilously close to the wind, King. You don't want a total embargo on your cargo, do you?'

Rodney had been practising a new gesture over the weekend. He raised his left eyebrow.

'ROD AGAINST RACISM I like,' said Fenton. 'ROD AGAINST THE BOMB is morally impeccable. However, NO FLIES ON ROD is another matter. When I told you to take the bloody things off your jacket I didn't mean that you should put them anywhere else. That scrum at break, round the coffee machine, was largely caused by your reading public, King, on its hands and knees, perusing your jeans. What the hell is that on the back of your neck?' Rodney turned round so that Fenton could see the badge on his collar: KING'S HEAD. NO COACHES.

'Exquisite lettering. I said nothing on your back, didn't I?'

'It's under my hair, unless I look down,' Rodney protested.

'It's under your *back* hair,' Fenton said. 'Edit yourself, King.'

Rodney edited himself drastically, removing KING CAN SERIOUSLY DAMAGE YOUR HEALTH, NO U TURNS, NO S BENDS, NO Y FRONTS and DANGER, CONCEALED EXIT from their carefully chosen sites, leaving only a striking model in severe black sans-serif on white, after the fashion of London Transport: WATCH THIS SPACE, which he wore until Wednesday.

WATCH THIS SPACE provoked a gratifying curiosity among his readership. Even Hobbers and his little harem displayed some interest in his frontage. When public response had, he judged, reached its peak, he removed WATCH THIS SPACE and pinned another badge in its place.

'Oh look – a new one,' Anna cried, homing in on it. A moment later she recoiled and walked back to Katy with an affronted expression.

'What does it say?' Katy asked. 'Something disgusting?'

'Read it yourself, if you want to know,' Anna said, sulkily. Katy stood up and approached Rodney's table. Rodney obligingly angled his shoulder the better to display his lapel. Katy leaned toward him, flushed, and backed off. Finally Liz, curious in spite of herself, wandered over.

'What does it say, Rod?'

'You wouldn't want to read it,' Rodney said, and folded his arms over his chest. 'I've got a different one for you.' He was aware of Hobbers, glowering over by the window. 'You can look at it later on.'

'Can't I see it now?'

'Not here.' Rodney looked shocked. 'See you at break – outside the library.' He rose swiftly and went out.

'Well then?' Hobbers demanded, with menaces, 'what did it say? What's his badge of the week or flavour of the month this time, then?'

'I don't know. He wouldn't let me look,' Liz said.

'You keep away from him and his badges,' Hobbers said. 'I don't know what the attraction is, the boring little git.'

'He's funny,' she said.

'*Funny?*'

'Anyway, attraction's not something you'd know much about, is it?' Liz said, shortly. She joined Katy and Anna on their way to class.

'Did you see what it said?' Katy asked.

'No. What did it say?'

'IF YOU CAN READ THIS YOU ARE TOO CLOSE,' Anna snapped.

Liz smiled. 'Oh.'

'What are you grinning about?'

'I suppose that's why he wouldn't let me read it,' Liz said.

At break she went to find Rodney outside the deserted library. He was there, his lapel vacant, and wearing a tie. On the knot of the tie was a badge.

'It better not be something foul,' Liz warned him.

Rodney mimed affronted innocence. Would I do that? asked his arching eyebrows.

Liz leaned toward him and studied the legend: READ THE SMALL PRINT. 'Is that all?'

'Of course it isn't. *Read* the small print.'

'I can see that. What small print?'

'Round the edge,' said Rodney.

'That?' Liz peered, inches away. 'That squiggle? I thought it was the border.'

'It's not a squiggle. It's small print: very small print.'

'Get away, I can't read that.'

'You can if you come near enough,' Rodney said, and held his breth, praying that he had not taken the onions out of last night's hamburger in vain.

'Is it going to be worth it?'

'It's for *you*.'

'And it's not something filthy?'

'Liz,' Rodney said, solemnly, 'if you don't trust me, you'll never find out what it says, will you?'

She was squinting past his chin, now. 'I still can't read it.'

'You'll have to come closer, then, won't you?' and he closed his eyes, saying silently, Oh God, make it work, and when he opened them again she was still there, right under his nose, reading the world's smallest love letter round the edge of his tenth badge. He thought, I wonder what would happen if I kissed her, and wished he could ask, but he had run out of badges.

Some ideas for writing

* Carry on with the story from the point where Jan Mark leaves it, with Liz's face right under Rodney's nose and Rodney wondering whether to kiss her. Look back in the story to work out whether he is likely to kiss her and how Liz is likely to react if he does. Will Hobbers, who has warned Liz to keep away from Rodney and his badges, appear in your bit of the story? Fenton has cut Rodney's badges down to one now, does this mean Rodney will have to find a new way to communicate?

* Write about the way Jan Mark makes this story funny. You may need to make some notes first on the different kinds of humour there are in the story, eg. what characters say, what they do, what the author says about them. Give examples from the story of each different kind of humour. Consider whether the author manages to describe funny aspects of school and add notes on these. Now write a rough draft of your essay on the kinds of humour in this story. Your conclusion should made it clear which bits of the story you find funny. After redrafting carefully write your final draft.

Statements of Account

Jenny Hursell

Jenny Hursell was born in Louth in Lincolnshire. Her first job was with the British Medical Association in London but she now lives on the Suffolk coast where she works part-time as Clerk to the Town Council. She has two daughters aged nine and thirteen. Eleven of Jenny Hursell's short stories have been broadcast on Radio 4 in the 'Morning Story' slot.

Statements of Account

Mandy's mother means well, she has her daughter's welfare at heart. However, this story shows how what is best for someone is not necessarily what they need. The story ends with Mandy having planned something which will hurt her mother and about which she can do nothing, in order to assert herself as an individual.

Statements of Account

'It's all right, Mandy, honest, you don't feel a thing. They just clamp your head in this Workmate thing, see, stick an ice cube behind your ear, get a darning needle and a mallet and then, wallop, it's done.' Mandy looked less than reassured; not that she took Karen seriously; her ears looked like a graveyard for redundant curtain rings so it couldn't hurt that much, else she'd not have kept going back, would she? Unless it was like having babies and you forgot. No, it wasn't the thought of the pain that bothered her. It was knowing what her mother would say.

'Eh, Mand, they're pretty,' Karen enthused. Mandy looked at the fine silver hoops dancing with enamelled butterflies. Yes, they were pretty, but she would have to choose something plainer. Perhaps her mother wouldn't mind too much then.

Karen moved towards the jeweller's door. 'You coming then, Mand? I haven't got all day you know. You chicken?'

'It's not that, Mandy protested. 'You know it's not that.'

'Yer Mum can't kill you can she? ... It's not as if you've gone and got yourself pregnant is it? Now that really would be stupid. They're your ears aren't they?'

Mandy looked at her friend. Mother couldn't stand Karen with her two-tone hair, her big boots and her lack of respect. She knew she'd blame Karen for her having her ears pierced and that was almost enough to put her off going through with it. She shut her eyes though; pictured herself, a shimmer of gold in each ear lobe and she knew she would feel good.

'Come on then,' she said. 'Let's go in.'

The shop assistant took them through to a stuffy room at the back, windowless and cluttered with boxes. Mandy wondered how clean it was.

'Choose what studs you fancy,' the girl said handing her a display card. 'I'll go wash my hands and get the gun.'

'Will she be doing it?' Mandy asked.

'Who'd you expect,' said Karen, 'a doctor? ... Come on, Mand, choose ... these hearts are nice ... but I wouldn't have those ruby ones. You'd look as if yer ear was bleeding.'

The girl returned with a battered vanity case from which she took a plastic bottle half-full of clear liquid and a metallic contraption that looked as though it might need a licence.

'I'd like some of these, please,' Mandy said indicating a pair of plain studs, and the girl slotted one into the gun. She up-ended the plastic bottle on a pink cotton-wool ball and dabbed at Mandy's ear lobes.

'Anaesthetic?' she queried hopefully.

'No ... antiseptic,' the girl replied. 'Don't bother to freeze yer ears now. It's so quick see. Not time for it to hurt ... Hold still.'

Zap! The thin metal shaft shot into her ear. Zap! And then the other one.

'Now, don't take them out for six weeks,' the girl impressed on her. 'Just dab 'em with the lotion and give 'em a daily twiddle ... like yer was winding yer watch up ... And don't wear heavy rings for four months else yer might split yer lobes.' Mandy shuddered. 'OK?' asked the girl.

'Yes, thank you,' Mandy whispered, and she looked at herself in the mirror the girl handed her.

'You look all right,' said Karen, who wasn't given to compliments.

'Yes,' said Mandy and smiled. She felt ... adorned.

As the shop bell jangled behind them she

stood for a moment in the doorway. And she did feel different, triumphant almost, like she had that morning she'd woken up to discover her first period had started. She touched the golden earrings gently to make sure they were still there.

'Feeling wobbly are you?' Karen asked, and Mandy nodded. 'They're a bit plain them ... get something fancy later, eh? Butterflies maybe or little elephants.'

Maybe, Mandy thought. But for the moment the studs were enough. She glanced boldly at her reflection in shop windows. She felt just as good as she'd thought she would. As she neared home though her euphoria sidled away. She knew her mother would be furious, and she knew she'd been devious. She hadn't deliberately disobeyed her mother because ... well, she'd never raised the matter with her, but she knew that if she had she'd have slapped the idea down straight-away, like she always did.

Her mother always had good reasons for saying no. Mandy's feelings did not stand a chance against her mother's reasons. No, she couldn't have white bread because it didn't have enough fibre; no, she was too young for high heels, they damaged unformed bones; no, she couldn't have a cat because they scratched the furniture and brought mice in; no, sweets were bad for the teeth, have some raisins; no, nail varnish looked tarty; no, she couldn't have a budgie, it might contract psittacosis; no, she couldn't go to the disco, it might make her deaf; and so on.

Mandy sighed. She was the only girl in her class who left home every morning wearing the full school uniform; it still gave her a thrill to pull on the pink ankle socks she kept in her school locker, for all that they looked ridiculous with her sensible shoes. When they got grubby Karen took them home and her Mum washed them. Mandy knew if her own mother found out she'd confiscate them because she wouldn't want her to get into trouble with her teachers. She meant it for the best, her mother did. She believed children nowadays had too much too easily and so she said 'no' as a matter of principle. It was character forming. And anyway she'd admitted once, saying 'no' gave you a breathing space and it was easier to change your mind. A 'yes' decision committed you to so much and it was difficult to withdraw from.

Mandy had learned that painful lesson early when she was five. She had so badly wanted a pet. The little boy down the road had been given a poodle. It looked like a black pom-pom on matchsticks and she'd ached to hold it. Her mother had said 'No, she couldn't have one; dogs leaked hairs all over and got ticks, and anyway she didn't need a dog.' But Mandy had employed all the cunning a five-year old can muster. She'd turned her wide, blue, woeful eyes on her grandmother and her grandmother had bought her a sheltie.

'She's a little Lassie,' Mandy had beamed. 'I can keep her, Mummy, can't I?'

Faced with a situation that she could do nothing about her mother had conceded on the understanding, however, that Mandy had to feed her, groom her, take her for walks.

'Oh, I will, Mummy, I will.'

They'd played together tirelessly, Mandy bearing with pride the pin-sharp assaults of Lassie's teeth and claws; she'd stroked and brushed away the tangles of their rough and tumble games until the dog's long coat had glowed like the amber depths of a waterfall in a Scottish burn. And she had taken her for walks but as she grew Lassie needed longer walks than Mandy could manage; she was boisterous too: several times she jerked the child over and careered joyfully unshackled around the park. Mandy had just picked herself up and raced after her, but mother had become increasingly concerned about the number of bruises and grazed knees.

One day she had announced that Daddy was going to London for a conference and that she had decided they should both go with him. 'We can visit the Science Museum, Amanda, and Buckingham Palace and the Zoo.' She had paused. 'And while we're away Lassie can have a little holiday too, in the country.' Mandy had thought Lassie would enjoy the country so they'd all bundled into the car and off they'd driven. It had seemed a long way. She'd kissed the dog and patted her and felt very sad to leave her, but it was only for a few days and she wouldn't have liked the escalators. And then half-way home her mother had said 'I've something to tell you, Amanda. You won't be seeing Lassie again. You couldn't manage her so I've given her away for good.'

She never explained for whose good; and they never went to London because Mandy couldn't stop her tears. Even eleven years later she tensed remembering the misery of those five-year old days. She'd never trusted her mother since and she'd always approached holidays and weekends with friends fearfully in case her mother should decide to give her away for good too. Now, as she fingered the trembling earrings she sensed that they weren't hers to keep either.

'Where've you been Amanda? You're late. I was worried.' Her mother lifted her head from her book. She noticed immediately.

'Take those out, Amanda.'

'But mother ...'

'Take them out ... you know precisely what I think about ear-piercing; it's barbaric ... self-mutilation ... Take them out. Take them out or I'll take them out for you ... This is Karen's doing no doubt.'

'It's nothing to do with Karen. It was my decision.'

'Take them out.' Her mother moved towards her, Mandy imagined her hand reaching up, ripping out the studs. She felt faint with rage and fear and frustration. She took out the earrings, clasped them tightly behind her back.

'Give them to me.'

'Please let me keep them.'

'How can I possibly let you keep them? You obviously can't be trusted not to wear them ... Give them to me.'

She loathed her mother at that moment. She handed over the studs, her eyes spiked with tears, and watched immobile as her mother took them away to the kitchen. The lid of the

Aga clanked and she knew then they'd gone, gone for good.

Karen thought she was mad. 'You'll regret it' she'd said. 'It's not like drawing on yourself with felt-tip pens. Once you've got 'em you can't get rid of 'em.'

'That's why I want one,' Mandy had replied.

'And it hurts,' Karen had gone on. 'It really hurts. My Dad got drunk when he had his. It's like having the TB jab over and over again only much worse.' She'd stared at Mandy. She'd seen she had made her mind up. 'Well I'm not coming with you,' she'd shouted. 'I'd be sick.'

Mandy recalled her friend's pained expression as she looked around the tattooist's parlour. She felt very calm. There were the bottles of stain, brilliant as milk-shake flavourings, the pattern books with curling corners, instruments strung aloft like Christmas poultry, photographs of satisfied customers their bodies swirling with mythical beasts and the names of loved ones. It looked scruffy and unhygienic, like the colourless man who was swabbing her arm.

'You are eighteen aren't you?' he said. She crossed her fingers and lied.

He yanked down one of the drill-like implements, flicked a switch.

'Don't you draw the design on first?' she asked.

He looked affronted. 'I'm an artist,' he said. 'And anyway I could do hearts with my eyes shut ... not that I will,' he reassured. 'But you might do best to shut yours, lassie.'

Lassie. Mandy clung onto the vision of the puppy with its piercing claws as the inky needle pistoned through her skin like a sewing machine, noisy as a cloud of wasps. It hurt more than she'd imagined. She bit her lip. He chatted about the weather, the merits of the four-two-four formation in football, Boy George and vandalism in the park. After twenty minutes he stopped. Her arm throbbed; but it bore a blue traceried outline like an embroidery transfer.

'Now comes the bit I really enjoy,' the man said. 'Colouring it in. Brings it to life.' And Mandy had neither the heart nor the nerve to say she'd had enough.

'Take deep breaths,' he advised; and the burning began again. When he'd finished she looked at her arm. It was a mess. The colours had all run together like on a child's watery painting. And then the man took a cloth and wiped it and the tattoo shone like a freshly-painted coat of arms.

'Keep it covered for a few days,' he said. 'Keep it clean and don't expose it to the sun for a fortnight . . . it'll form lots of little scabs. Don't pick 'em. They'll go septic.'

She walked home in a dream. Her arm felt sore, scalded, but she felt . . . proud. Initially she'd planned to show it to her mother; but she hadn't done it out of spite. It was for herself and as the weeks trailed by she treasured the secret knowledge of her tattoo. Somehow it had made everything easier to bear, had made a space for herself, knowing that she had made a decision that could not be unmade.

On the first day of the holidays she slept late and mother took her up a cup of tea. As she reached out for the cup her sleeve rippled treacherously up her arm.

'That's a nasty bruise, Amanda.' Mandy glanced at the tattoo and quickly shook down her sleeve; but why? She peeled it back again, assertively held out her arm and watched, pleasure in her achievement salted with pity as the tattoo and its message registered:
For mother, with love.

Some ideas for writing

* Retell this story from the mother's point of view. Obviously you will have to leave some bits out, like having the tattoo done (because she wasn't there) but you will need to make more of other bits, like her reaction to the tattoo.

* Write about the mother/daughter relationship described in this story. What kind of relationship is it? Why does Mandy rebel? Who do you sympathise with, the mother or the daughter? What could have been done to make the relationship better? Back up points you make with evidence from the story.

MAUREEN

Michael Rosen

Michael Rosen lives in Hackney, London with four children, Eddie, Joe, Naomi and Laura. The Holloway Road is quite near where he lives and he has travelled up and down it for years which is why *Maureen* is set there. Michael Rosen has worked as a writer in residence in many schools, both primary and secondary. He has also appeared on Channel 4 as Dr Smartypants.

Other Knockouts by Michael Rosen are *Nasty!* and *The Bakerloo Flea*.

Maureen

This story could just be read as a straightforward amusing account of the escape and recapture of a dangerous animal in a busy part of London. Looked at this way it is an easy story. However, the strange way that the story has been told adds extra interest. We call this the structure of the story.

Most stories are told by a narrator. Often the narrator seems to be the same person as the author. Sometimes the author choses quite a different person to be the narrator (eg. someone younger or of the opposite sex.) In this story Michale Rosen has a narrator – the 'I' who begins the story. This narrator is male – the keeper calls him 'Sir' at the end of the story. The narrator sounds like Micheal Rosen himself except at the very end when the narrator tells himself that the story about Maureen must be true. At the end the author (Michael Rosen) seems to be telling the reader that the narrator is foolish to believe the story about Maureen. The story about Maureen was not told by the narrator – it was told to him by the Bakerloo Flea Woman. (She is called this because the first story she ever told was about a flea on the Bakerloo Line on the London Underground.)

The reader is left not knowing who to believe, as the story reaches us at third hand – told by the Bakerloo Flea Woman to the narrator written by the author (who made the whole thing up anyway!)

Maureen

I was in London Zoo the other day. I've got a season ticket and I like to look at the animals when no one else is there. Like in winter. Have you seen the polar bear? It paces to and fro along this rock and then every now and then it dives into the freezing water. You'd die if you went in there. When it gets out, it shakes all the water off. I was watching this when I heard a voice behind me go, 'Have you seen my mate over there?' I looked around and it was the Bakerloo Flea Woman.

'Oh hallo,' I said. 'I was just looking at the polar bear.'

'Yeah,' she said, 'you ought to take a gander at the grizzlies. My mate's in there.'

'Oh,' I said, 'you know one of the zoo keepers do you?'

'No,' she says.

'Who's your mate, then?' I said.

'One of the grizzlies,' she says.

'Oh yes. And what's he called?' I said.

'Maureen,' she says.

'Right then,' I said. 'Take me to meet her.'

So off we went, past those goat things with the twisty horns and that horrible vulture that stands there ripping at bits of old flesh. Actually, its neck looks like bits of old flesh as well. Over to the grizzlies. The grizzly bears. 'There she is. Maureen.' And then she called to her, 'Maureen! Maureen!'

And there in the corner of the bears' pen is a great big grizzly. I looked at it. Its eyes rolled over towards us.

'See,' said the Bakerloo Flea Woman, 'she knows me.'

'Knows you, my foot,' I said. 'She does that to everyone. Right watch this,' I said. 'What's she called, did you say? Maureen?'

'That's it,' she says.

'Right,' I said. 'MAUREEN! MAUREEN!'

Well, all Maureen did at that was lick her foot.

'See,' said the Bakerloo Flea Woman. 'She only looks up for me.'

'All right,' I said. 'How do you know her then?'

'Now you're asking,' she says. 'You're not going to stand here in the freezing cold and hear this one out, are you? Let's go over to the cafe.'

So off we went, past the gorillas sulking in

their house, past the gibbons whooping around like kids gone mad on an adventure playground. We went into the cafe and we were the only people in there apart from a young couple looking into each other's eyes and trying to drink one cup of coffee at the same time.

'Right,' she says. 'Maureen. Well, it all starts with the buses. You see, old Maureen, she nearly got run over by one.'

'By a bus?' I said.

'Yep,' she said.

'They don't drive buses round the zoo, do they?' I said.

'No. In London. A double-decker bus in the Holloway Road.'

I tried to picture it. A huge grizzly bear walking across the Holloway Road with a double-decker bus zooming past it. No. Couldn't be true.

'You see, son,' she said. 'I was a clippy – bus conductress to you – on the 43 – among others. On this particular day the crew was me and Lloyd. A day much like any others, coming down the Holloway Road. Shopping day for many round the old Holloway Arcade, Jones Brothers and all that, under the railway bridge at Holloway Road Station. I was on top, on the upper deck, right up the front, collecting fares off about five kids who were busy driving the bus to Mars or somewhere. Then there's this big kid, easily fifteen, and he's with the younger ones and he goes, "Half to Highbury Corner."

"You're never a half," I says.

"Am," he goes.

"Come on son. Don't mess me about." And I held out my hand and did my I'm-getting-fed-up look out the window.

'Well, just as I looked up, I saw that in front of us was this whopping great big lorry. Nothing strange in that, except just as I am looking at it, the back doors slowly opened out towards us. And just as I was thinking, Lloyd's going to give the feller driving the waggon a zig on his lights or something, this great fat grizzly bear rolled out the back of the lorry on to the Holloway Road. Right in front of us.

'Of course, the kids went spare. "It's a bear. IT'S A BEAR." And it certainly weren't no person dressed up. First thing it does is stand up on its rear legs and it looks about ten foot tall. Then it opens its mouth in a great big yawn and you can see right down its throat, teeth, tongue, tonsils, the lot. It must have been about two foot from Lloyd's nose, in the cab down below me.

'Then, of course, everyone on top with me is crowding to the front of the bus. They all want to get a sight of it. "It's a bear. It's a bear," they keep shouting.

'Well, of course it doesn't just stand there. It turned. Maybe it thought it could get back into the lorry, but the doors had swung back. Of course, the fellers driving the lorry knew nothing about it.

'But then it starts loping up by the side of the lorry. Can you imagine, sitting in the cab of a lorry thinking you've got a grizzly bear safe and sound in the back when suddenly it's standing there looking at you through the window? Well that didn't last long. Next thing it does is cross the road towards Holloway Road Station.

'Of course by now, there's cars hooting and people screaming and the road is clearing like a bomb's just about to go off. Cars are reversing down the Holloway Road, up the Holloway Road, and of course people are jumping off my bus and scarpering. Off they went, some of them leaving behind their bags of fruit and veg. and what-have-you. They'd probably have been safer staying on board. I think it was the sight of seeing everybody else bunking off that got them going. Once two or three were running, so was the rest. Most of them belted off down beside the college there. The fellers driving the lorry pulled it into the side and got out.

'For a moment it seemed like it was just them, us and the bear. I was downstairs by now. I looked behind us and it was one of those days that the buses get all clogged up together. And there was about four of five of us – not all 43's of course, standing there.

'Well, the grizzly by now had lurched back to our side of the road again. Well, I'll never know what made Lloyd do it, but blow me doesn't he start the bus running forwards towards the bear? And the moment he does that, I'm shouting to Frank in the bus behind. He must have known what was going on by now.

"Follow us," I shouted. "We can trap it."

'Goodness knows what made me say it. And goodness knows what made Frank agree, but there's now two buses making off down the Holloway Road after this huge great big grizzly bear.

'Well, like I said, the road's clear by now. But the sight of these two giant red buses coming up to it sent the bear off down the road. And on we went. The other buses following after, trundling along after the bear, down the Holloway Road. And the third and fourth buses are spreading out across the road and we're taking up the whole Holloway Road, both sides, and the old bear is loping along ahead of us.

'On we went, past the Brewery Tap – that's a pub. It's not going to poke its nose in there, is it? I thought, and go "Half a lager, mate". No, on it went. Past the old Arsenal cafe that isn't there any more. It's not going to go in there is it? You know a bit of the old "Cuppa tea, mister," "Sorry, we don't serve Spurs supporters or bears." No none of that either. And on it went. Past the Kebab joints, didn't stop for a quick doner. And there's people cowering in the doorways of their shops, looking out of windows. You'd've thought we was the Queen. And that old bear looks like it's enjoying itself. I mean it's really getting a chance to stretch its old legs. And it's moseying up to the Keep Left sign on the island in the middle of the road. Next, it's ambled across the road to poke its nose into the big catering place. Probably saw its reflection in the window, but for one moment it looked like it was going to go in there and order one hundred and forty dinners for a wedding reception or something.

'Then as we trundle on down towards it, it comes to the big motor-cycle joint. Maybe it's going to hop on a Honda, next, I thought. Imagine it, a grizzly bear zooming down the Holloway Road on a Honda. Then before we know it, we're at Highbury Corner. Now, Highbury Corner, I don't know whether you know it, it's not really a corner at all. It's a great big roundabout. The CB people call it Highbury Doughnut. In the middle of it, it's like a little park. Trees, grass, bushes, flowers and stuff. So there's us coming down past Highbury and Islington station. People rushing into the post office to hide, running off to Highbury Fields.

'And of course, the same thing's happening up the streets that feed into Highbury Corner. Cars are turning round and reversing away. People are getting into safe places to watch and the buses are left standing there. Well, I don't know if it was the sight of our four or five buses coming down the Holloway Road together, or what, but the buses down all the other roads, Upper Street and all that, they start moving in towards the big Highbury Corner Round about as well.

'So, suddenly there's about twelve of us. Twelve double-decker buses. Well, the old bear must have thought something was happening because it was like we was surrounding that park space in the middle. A great red ring of buses.

'Now, there's a fence round the roundabout. And what with our buses closing in, and the sight of the green leaves and flowers on the roundabout, the bear climbs the fence and was in. I don't suppose the men from the council ever thought when they were building that fence that it'd have to stand the weight of a two-ton grizzly.

'So now, the grizzly bear was on the inside and we were on the outside. What I didn't know, though, was that those two fellers driving the truck that had the bear in, they had hopped on one of our buses. Somewhere along the line the police had got to hear of it, all the fire services and the zoo-emergency people and for all I know there was a gang of SAS men on red alert, RAF helicopters and goodness knows what.

'So next thing, the drivers and the keepers are at the fence, looking in. The bear had quietened down by now, it was just snuffling about in the bushes. One of the keepers was calling out to it. That was the first time I heard its name.

"Maureen," he goes, "Maureen."

'I thought "Maureen." Now, you'd never have known it was Maureen to look at her, would you? Fancy that.

'Well, not long after that, the zoo people did their bit with them drug pellets, shooting it and the old bear keeled over and went to sleep. And that was the end of that.

'They had to use the pellets. I mean no one

was going to go up to it and go, "Look here Maureen, would you like to walk back to your lorry now? Sorry the doors fell open, but we'll lock them next time ..."

'So then they had to get this thing like a breakdown-truck to hoist her up and stick her in the lorry. To tell the truth I didn't stick around to see all that, but I'm told it took about twenty grown men to push old Maureen in there. Then they carted her off to the zoo. Here. Of course, the papers next day were full of it. MAUREEN'S DAY OUT and MAUREEN'S REMOVALS and there were pictures of her being hoisted into the truck and all that.

'Sad to say, none of them got the picture I wanted to see. It would have been like a picture from high-up; a picture of Highbury Corner surrounded with all our buses and in the middle old Maureen, snuffling though the council flower beds. I mean it was us in our buses that cornered it, wasn't it? All the rest was drug-guns and breakdown-trucks and all that. Oh well, not to worry, I just have to carry the picture of it round in my head. I can always come in here and have a look at her.'

'That's very nice,' I thought.

'It'll break my heart when she dies, mind,' she said.

'Look,' I said, 'I've got to go. I'm going to

have one more look at her myself, now you've told me all this. You coming?'

'No.'

So I went off to look at Maureen. I was standing there looking at her, Maureen herself, when the keeper came out of the little door of the bear's pen.

So I says to him, 'You've been feeding Maureen, have you?'

And he looks at me and goes, 'You what?'

'You've been feeding Maureen, have you?'

'No,' he said. 'I've been feeding the bears.'

'Well, isn't that one Maureen?' I said.

'No,' he said, 'That's Samson.'

'What about that one?' I said, pointing to the other one.

'That's Betty.' he said.

'Well, where's Maureen?' I said.

So he said, 'You tried the shop, Sir? People who get lost often go there, sir.'

I suddenly realised he thought I was some kind of a nutter. I said, 'You ever looked after a bear in here called Maureen?'

'Not in the last six years, we haven't. I'm sorry sir, I can't hang about' and off he went. He was probably glad to get away from me.

So I went back to where the Bakerloo Flea Woman was. I was going to tell her it wasn't

Maureen. It was Samson and Betty. But she wasn't there.

'Oh well,' I thought. 'Just as well. It wouldn't be right, somehow to tell her that her bear wasn't really the same one that fell off the back of a lorry. Unless ... unless she'd made the whole thing up. No she wouldn't have. Everything else she's told me is true, isn't it?'

Some ideas for writing

* Write a story of your own which was told by someone else to your narrator (who must be different from you, the author). The story could be about a dangerous animal which has escaped in the area where you live.

* Explain in as much detail as you can how the story would have changed if Michael Rosen had been on the bus following Maureen's lorry and had narrated the story of her escape and recapture himself. You will need to re-read the story carefully making notes as you do so in order to do this properly.

THE CENTRE

Adèle Geras

Adèle Geras was born in Jerusalem. Her early childhood was spent in many countries, including North Borneo and the Gambia. She has had several jobs including being a singer, an actress and a French teacher. She now lives in Manchester with her husband and two daughters, Sophie and Jenny. She has had sixteen books published.

The Centre

Adèle Geras has taken a very ordinary place, a shopping centre, and made it unusual and frightening. She has laid clues to help the reader guess what the ending will be. She hasn't spelt out exactly what happened at the end but has left the reader to do some work. The newspaper reports are there to explain the background to the story quickly and to make the events seem more real and believeable.

The Centre

> *From The Evening Gazette: October 25th*
>
> Elmdale Police are mounting a city-wide hunt for young Stuart Windell (13), who disappeared last Saturday afternoon.
>
> ## *Distraught*
>
> 36 year-old Mrs Brenda Windell, the boy's mother, said this morning, 'We are all really distraught. This is not like Stuart at all. He went into town on Saturday to spend a record token. If anyone has seen him, please, please get in touch with the Police. No one will be angry with him. We just want him back.'
>
> ## *Baffled*
>
> Chief Inspector Frank Davis confessed himself baffled. 'We have interviewed Stuart's friends and scores of shoppers. Quite a few people think they remember seeing him in the Ashfield Centre on Saturday afternoon.'

> 13 year-old Andrew Roberts, Stuart's best friend, told the Gazette reporter, 'Stu didn't catch the bus home with us. He said he was going to look around a bit. We didn't think anything of it. We just went home. I wish we hadn't now.'
>
> ## Third in a series?
>
> Chief Inspector Davis refused to comment on the possibility that Stuart's disappearance was the third in a series of such happenings. A nationwide search has failed to find 10 year-old Elisabeth Lacey who was last seen on August 20th and there has been no news of 12 year-old Tracy Walsh, who vanished in May of this year.
>
> ## Is the centre safe?
>
> All three children were last seen at the Ashfield Centre, which prompts the Evening Gazette to ask: is the Centre, (opened last year and regarded by many as the most advanced shopping precinct in Europe) really safe, in spite of Police presence during the daytime and a regular night patrol? (see page 6 for Editorial comment.)

The Desk Sergeant had recognised Ted the minute he'd walked into the station: old Ted Rees, four layers of clothes on top of countless layers of dirt and the whole lot walking along in a fog of stale booze and cigarettes.

'... a word with ... Chief Inspector Davis ... That's right,' he was saying.

The young policeman sighed and looked as severely as he could at the old tramp standing before him. 'Ted,' he said. 'I'm sure you've got a lot to say to the Chief, but now's not the time. We're busy, see? Got a lot on our plates, know what I mean? Whyn't you go back to the Centre where you belong and have a look at the televisions in Philip's window? Go on, there's a good chap.'

Ted sniffed, shuffled his feet and muttered, 'Been watching it, haven't I? Why I'm here. That, and the paper, like. Gissa fag, Sarge, and I'll tell you. Doesn't have to be the Chief. Tell you all about it.'

'Let's be having it then,' said the policeman. 'Got nothing on at all, I haven't. Just ready for a bedtime story, I am. Go on, I'm sitting comfortably ...'

'What about the fag though? Can't think right at this time of day, not without a smoke.'

'Don't smoke, though, do I? Filthy habit. Come on, either you tell your tale and get out or you just get out. Which is it going to be?'

Ted hesitated, turned to go.

'Don't know if I'll bother ... wanted to see the Chief, really, like ... about that kid ... the one that's gone missing ...'

No magician uttering abracadabra ever

effected a speedier transformation. The Desk Sergeant shot out from behind his desk, and within five minutes, Ted Rees found himself sitting at a table drinking a cup of tea and eating Digestive biscuits. Across the table from him was the Chief: Chief Inspector Frank Davis himself.

'Grand,' Ted chuckled. 'That was grand. Do a nice cuppa tea in this nick, I'll say that for you. You haven't got a fag on you, have you? Finish the tea off a treat, a fag would.'

Chief Inspector Davis threw a packet of cigarettes and a box of matches down on to the table.

'Use your saucer for an ashtray. And start talking. I haven't got all day, you know.'

Ted smiled. 'Ain't half long, these fags aren't. When they're not dog-ends. Used to dog-ends, meself.'

'I'm sorry I couldn't get you any then,' Chief Inspector Davis muttered through clenched teeth. 'Now. Let's be having you. You seen the boy, or what?'

'No. Ain't seen him. He's gone, in't he? No one's seen him. That's the point.'

'Then what the bloody hell are you wasting Police time for? Thought you said you had information, you dirty old bundle of rubbish. Get out, go on, get out.'

'I never said I hadn't got information. Only that I hadn't seen him. I have got information ...'

Chief Inspector Davis sighed. 'Start at the beginning.'

'Right,' Ted coughed. 'D'you remember what used to be there down Market Road before they put up that Centre?'

'Shops,' the Chief Inspector said. 'What's this got to do with anything?'

'I'm coming to that.' Ted picked a Digestive crumb from his beard and chewed it thoughtfully. 'Do you remember Clevely's?'

'Clevely's? Dress shop, or drapers or what have you? I must have walked past it a thousand times I suppose. What about it?'

'Ever met Ma Clevely, what ran it?'

'No, and I don't care if I never do. Listen mate, if you think you're going to sit there puffing at your bleeding Bensons and gossiping about shopkeepers, you've got another think coming ...'

'Keep your hair on ... it's all ... what's that word ... revelant.'

'Relevant.'

'Yes. Relevant. Just listen while I tell you. This Ma Clevely was a terror. Had a lot of young girls out at the back of the shop, sewing away for dear life. Sweated labour, it was. I say she was a terror, 'cos she's dead. Them closing her shop and all. Putting up that pile of shoeboxes, that's what did for her. Mind, she was old. I'm not saying she wasn't. I can remember a time, before you were born, oh yes, when all the gentry, all the ladies went there for dresses and suits and such. They had kiddies' clothes too. I had a top hat from there once.'

'You never had a top hat in your life, you old fraud.'

Ted glared at the Chief Inspector. 'Didn't get born a tramp, though, did I? What do you know about it anyway? But Ma Clevely ... they had to throw her out you know. It was in the papers. But I saw it. They chucked out all the dummies and stuff, clothes and that, into the van that was waiting on the pavement, and she was stood there screaming. Saying she'd be back. Saying she'd have her shop again, ranting and raving like she was drunk ...'

'Is this getting us anywhere?' Chief Inspector Davis had stopped making notes.

'I'm coming to what I want to say ... This is it ...' He paused and took the cigarette out of his mouth, and leaned forward.

'I reckon she's back there. Back in that Centre.'

'I thought you said she was dead ...'

'She is ...'

'What's this then? You've seen her ghost? Is that it? You've been wasting everyone's time with a spooky little story out of your drink-fuddled brain. Go on, get out of here. Just go. I've had enough.'

Ted Rees stood up. 'I haven't seen her. But I can tell, Chief. She's there, all right. And I reckon it's her what took them kids.'

'And what's she supposed to have done with them? Set them sewing invisible clothes on invisible machines in a bloody non-existent shop? Go on, clear off out of here before I book you as drunk and disorderly.'

It was drizzling as Ted Rees left the Police Station and made his way back to the Ashfield Centre. No drizzle in there, he thought. No air, no sunshine, but no drizzle either. There was that much to be said for it.

'Do we have to go, Mum?' Sharon Windell hesitated at the door. 'Do we really have to?' 'Do you think I like it any better than you? Don't you think I'd rather stay away when it all reminds me of him ...?' Brenda Windell sniffed, 'but I've got no choice, have I? I'm not getting you a coat somewhere else when I've got ten pounds credit at Brink's, am I?'

'No, I suppose not.' Sharon sighed as they left the house.

'Anyway,' she said, 'may be this time we'll ...'

'No, Sharon, we won't.' Her mother shook her head. 'I used to think like that. Every phone call, every knock at the door, I used to hope and pray, but now it's nearly a month and I've stopped hoping ... someone would have seen him if he were alive ...'

Sharon thought: but if he were dead, there'd be his body, wouldn't there? I don't believe it. I don't believe he's dead. They can all say what they like, the police and everything, but if he were dead, I'd know. I'd feel it inside. And I don't. There's an emptiness inside me. If Stu were dead there wouldn't be an emptiness. There'd be a hurt, an awful hurt like claws, tearing me.

Walking through the Ashfield Centre with her mother, Sharon felt that nothing in it was real. For a start, there was no real light, only a blueish brightness about the air that sucked the colour from people's cheeks so that everyone looked pale. The light never changed either, not like outside. There, it was sunny or dull, day or night, dawn, sunset, moonlight even, and here –

nothing: a pale neon nothing, the kind of light that didn't even make shadows. The air smelled of plastic. Cold and heat never penetrated the Centre. Neither did rain or sunshine. What you heard was noise, but no voices. Disembodied loudspeaker announcements, frantic music spilling out of shops, the same tired water being pumped up out of the fountains, splashing half-heartedly on to rubbery plants. Sharon set herself to count the people who were smiling. She didn't see any, unless she was going to include the shrieking bands of boys and girls not much older than Stu, trying to look as if they were having a good time, making the walkways ring to the clatter of their hard, hard shoes. Later, sitting with her mother on a yellow plastic bench, looking at the people walking by, she was suddenly struck by their sameness. It was as though every time she came here the identical crowd was waiting for her. They belonged to the Centre, Sharon decided. They were a part of it, not real people from outside at all, just a breed of mechanical Centre-people who lived there, stayed there always, a part of it. As much a part of it as the escalators and the litter bins and the wooden animals for the children to climb on. And Stu had become one of them, she was sure of it. The more she thought about it, the more plausible it seemed to her. He had been absorbed by the Centre, sucked in to become one of its people. That was why no one had found his body: because he was here. Here where she was. And if she looked carefully, she realized with a sudden racing of the heart, she might find him ...

'Mum, can we walk about a bit more? I want to look at the shops.'

'Really? I thought you hated this place. I know I do. Still, if you want to ...'

They walked and walked and Sharon peered at every face as she passed it. There was no sign of her brother. But I know he's here, she thought, as they made their way out of the Centre and into the street. I'll go and tell the Police. They'll know what to do.

'Well now, Sharon.' Chief Inspector Davis smiled his 'I'm-being-kind-to-a-child' smile. 'That's all very interesting, you know, but I assure you it's not true. You see, dear, we've checked everything. Already. And I promise you, at the end of every day, everyone leaves the Centre and the whole place is locked up and there's only the night-watchman. Really. I wouldn't lie to you, now would I?'

Sharon shook her head.

'Now I'll get my sergeant to take you home in a police car, Sharon. How would you like that?'

'No, you mustn't. I mean, thanks, but I'll take the bus. My mum doesn't know I've come to see you. She thinks I'm at Francine's house. Thanks for the drink.'

After she had gone, Chief Inspector Davis shook his head in amazement. The things these kids came up with. Honestly. Whatever next . . . all the people in the Centre, not real . . . it's television that's responsible, he thought. Feed them a lot of imaginary rubbish and here's what happens. Can't sort out what's real and what isn't. Still (Chief Inspector Davis prided himself on his awareness of modern psychology) the poor little kid had been under a lot of strain, what with her brother gone missing and liable to turn up dead one day. Perhaps it made it easier to think . . . anything at all.

Sharon hid in the belly of the huge wooden rhino and waited. She was nervous, but it was a good plan and she had to carry it through or she would never know . . . Francine was in the plan. She's my alibi, thought Sharon. I'm supposed to be spending the night at her house. Francine's mum and dad are going out tonight. Right at this very minute the baby-sitter thinks I'm up in Francine's room ... we made a shape out of pillows to put in the other bed. We practised. I'll go back first thing in the morning. I wonder what time they open this place up ... Sharon looked at her watch. Eight o'clock. She peeped out of the rhino. The Centre was empty. All the big lights had been turned off, but shop lights still shone out on to the marble. The silence filled her ears, deafened her. She had heard the night watchman earlier, walking about, but he had gone now. That was one good thing about marble floors – you could hear someone coming from a long way away, and going back to wherever they came from as well. No one would hear her though. She had worn her trainers especially.

She climbed down out of the rhino, and began to walk slowly along a walkway that seemed to stretch on forever, staying very close to the shop windows, as if the colourless light could banish the fear, as if the models inside could reach out plastic arms for comfort. The fountains had been turned off. The plants were black near the black water. Twice, she heard the night watchman and hid behind a bench and looked at him. He seemed very old and frail to be a guard. Just an old man, really, but it pleased her that he was there somewhere, ready to give help if she needed it. Another human being in a desert of stone and half-light and silence. Sharon crept down the unmoving escalator to that part of the Centre which lay below ground level. She and her mother hardly ever came down here: all the big stores were upstairs, but Sharon felt she had to look everywhere. I won't find anything, she thought. I must be mad. Chief Inspector Davis was right. All the people who come here are ordinary people and they all go home at night to their houses and there's nothing here at all but silence and this dim light and shops ... and those animals and the night watchman. She leaned her forehead against a shop window and something caught her eye. It was a shoe. A trainer, just like Stu's The dummy in the window was wearing trainers just like Stu's. She shivered. There was nothing strange about that. Perhaps the shop sold trainers. She looked more closely. It couldn't be. It was. A pink stain on the white part of the shoe, like the stain she'd made spilling Ribena on Stu's trainers the first week he'd had them. She would never forget his anger, nor the shape of the mark that was left after Mum had scrubbed them: like a lopsided heart. A crooked heart-shaped stain and there it was right in front of her in the window. She raised her eyes a little, hardly daring to look ... and there he was, or a dummy that was dressed in his clothes ... Sharon pressed herself up against the window to see better. They were Stu's clothes, she was sure of that. And the dummy ... the dummy looked like her brother. How had they done it? Why? Who would want to? And where was Stu if this model boy was wearing his clothes? Sharon knew at once what she had to do – get into the shop and get the clothes off the plastic limbs of that doll and take them to the police. They'd know. They'd have tests they could do to show that the clothes were Stu's. I'll have to break the glass, she thought, and then: if I do, I'll get into trouble. I'd better find the night watch-man, call out to him, he'll understand. Everyone will understand when they see what I've found. Mum and Dad and Francine's parents – no one will be cross. This is clues. This will help them find out what's happened to Stu. She glanced at the dummy again and was just plucking up courage to shout into all the silence and break it, when she heard the footsteps far away and dived into the tiny space of the shop doorway, flattening herself against the glass, her heart beating so loudly that the pulse filled her head. The sound of the footsteps was nearer now. Tap, tap, swish. Tap, tap, swish on the marble like a lady in a long, silky dress. It can't be, Sharon thought. It's the night watchman. And I want him to come. I do. I was going to call him. Closer ... tap, tap, swish ... and closer. Sharon left the doorway and stepped out to see who was coming. High-ceilinged passages stretched away to both sides of her ... she could see and see and see for what looked like miles. No one. Nothing at all. Just a sound. Tap, tap, swish ... closer and closer. Louder and louder.

'Who is it?' Sharon tried to scream, but it came out a croak, almost a whisper. 'What do you want? Who are you?' Her own voice bounced back from the silence all around her. 'There's a night watchman, you know. He'll get you! He will ... Help!'

Tap, tap, swish. Nearer. Almost on top of her. Darkness came down over Sharon's eyes and she turned and ran. She didn't know where she was running to ... part of her mind knew she must find the guard, yell and scream, attract attention, but her body said run, hide, keep silent, get away, escape.

At her back the footsteps gathered speed. She could hear hoarse panting behind her, almost at her shoulder, and she ran and ran, blindly, thinking only of the unmoving silver escalator, thinking of getting up, up, out of this underground place, away from the terrible swishing and the laboured breathing ... away anywhere. There it was. The escalator. Sharon lunged towards it and almost flew up the steps. At the top, she stumbled and fell. Can't fall. Get up. Can't stop. It's coming. Get up. Coming nearer. Up. Sharon crawled to her feet and began to run again, half-covering her eyes with her hands because she couldn't bear to look again and see nothing. Up here. The watchman must be here. Sharon found her voice.

'Stop it. Please help ... help me ...' Sound tore itself from her throat, which was blocked and filled with terror and the exhaustion of running and running and not stopping for breath.

'Where are you? Please ... I'm sorry for being here ... please. Come and save me ... Oh, I can't ... I can't run any more.'

But she ran, because it was there ... tap, tap, swish ... so near. Not a swish, a rustle. Like petticoats ... so close now. And breathing and something else. A smell, like old face powder ... old perfume ... stale, stale and old ... horrible. Run, fly away, hide. Where to hide in all the marble and the glass? The Rhino, Sharon thought. I must get to the Rhino. There it was. Wooden. Hollow. Somewhere to hide till someone comes. She ran, stumbled, crawled along, unable to breathe properly any more, until she reached it. Her head was full of footsteps and rustling and in her nostrils the smell ... stronger now. Violets. It made her want to vomit. She fell against the smooth wooden feet of the rhino and climbed into the opening of its belly. There was a small platform inside. Sharon curled up with her hands wrapped round her head to shut out the sounds, and her knees touching her face, breathing in her own smell, the smell of her jeans and her own sweat, trying to blot out that other smell ... Minutes passed. Sharon listened. Silence. No more footsteps. I'll wait, she thought, and then I'll look. I'll look out of the top. She lay trembling, crying, cold with fear for ten minutes timed on her watch, and then she slowly uncurled and stood up ... at once the smell flew up at her face, stronger than ever, as if it were a live thing lying in wait for her outside the rhino's body. She ducked down and curled up again on the platform, pressing herself against the wood, wishing she could become a part of it, melt into it, stop being herself, disappear dissolve ... The wooden walls all round her seemed softer, wrapped her and enfolded her, and in her ear came a whisper ... sleep, sleep, and Sharon closed her eyes. Sleep ... forget ... don't run away any more, don't hide any more, just sleep. Close your eyes and sleep. Sleep and dream. Dream.

This is a dream. I know it is, because everything is wavy. The air is rippling like water, breaking into patterns, swirls of light and shadow and nothing is hard. Even wood is soft, like flesh ... and I'm not afraid. Hands, gloved hands are touching me, gentle hands. I'm being pulled out of somewhere ... lifted, yes, like a baby ... arms are lifting me, but I can't feel the arms ... carrying me. I can hear somebody walking ... tap, tap, swish ... and smell violets ... lovely ... soft, powdery smell. Looking up. I'm looking up and lights are slipping by over my head slowly, and slowly and then more quickly, and then no more lights. Darkness and a bed ... or a table, with a sheet on it, and then someone is stroking me, like a cat, stroking ... a cat's tail, but it's wet ... stroking my arms and my feet and in between my fingers, and my face ... wetness all over my face ... lips, nose, cheeks all wet. I want to touch my face but my arm is heavy. I can't move it. I want to turn my head. My head won't turn.

I'm stiff. All stiff and cold. I can't move at all. Only my eyes. Hands lift me. I can't feel hands, but I'm lifted. Standing. The light is white ... eyes hurt ... can't move head. No more moving ... don't need to move. Stuart is next to me. He can't move. But we can see. See each other. Not move, but see each other always. Stay like this. Stiff. Always.

Ted Rees looked at the photograph in the newspaper and sighed. He looked at it again and then threw it away in the litter bin. Poor little thing. First the brother and now her. I've seen her before somewhere. Where, though, that's the thing? Where was it now? It's hard to remember, but I seen her. Ma Clevely's got her, that's what. Bloody coppers. She's here, 'cos I heard her and I smelled her and I know and she's got her. All of them, probably, and I seen them, but I don't know ... it's hard to remember. Poor little kid ... Poor Ted ... maybe when I get sober I'll remember again ... never know yer luck.

The old tramp propped himself against the shop window and looked in. Then he started laughing. Choking and laughing and coughing and making such a noise that the Centre policeman was forced to give him a warning:

'Come on, Ted. Can't have this row, you know. Scares everyone off, doesn't it? Can't see what's so bleeding funny anyhow.'

'It's him, see. That boy doll in that window. He's got a wine stain on that fancy shoe of his. Just like me. I got one and all. Wanna have a look?'

The policeman led Ted away, still laughing.

Some ideas for writing

* Write a horror story of your own set in an ordinary familiar place. Keep the reader guessing about what is going on but give clues to the ending.

* Write the article that appears in The Evening Gazette after the mystery of the disappearing school children has been solved. Make it look and sound as much like a real newspaper account as you can. Look back at the newspaper cutting that starts the story. You will need to work out exactly what you think happened to do this properly.

THE CONSETT GIANTS

Terry Deary

Terry Deary is a Teacher Advisor in English and Drama to Sunderland schools. He writes for young people in his spare time and holidays. Since he began writing in 1975 he has had twenty books published in Britain and three in America. When he is not writing he enjoys producing plays, reading thrillers, playing cricket for his village team, supporting Sunderland Football Club or rebuilding the old pub where he lives with his family and their horses, sheep, dogs and cats.

Other Knockouts by Terry Deary are *Twist of the Knife, Walking Shadows, I met her on a rainy day, Don't dig up your granny when she's dead, The Ice House of Nightmare Avenue, The Treasure of Skull Island* and *Spine Chilling Stories.*

The Consett Giants

A tall story is an exaggerated story that you are not really expected to believe. The way the author begins this story shows that he doesn't really expect you to believe it. However, stories like this are often told to explain why bits of the world look the way they do. (You may remember stories like this from when you were younger which explained how animals came to

THE CONSETT GIANTS

look as they do, eg. how the tortoise got its shell, how the leopard got its spots.) This fantastic story about three giants is told to explain how the towns of Corbridge, Benfieldside and Consett got their names; why there is a hollow in the ground at Howden; and how the ironworks at Consett came to be built and then run down. A tall story is also designed to entertain.

The Consett Giants – A tall story

So, you don't believe in giants, eh?

Well, I'll admit that there aren't a lot of them around these days.

But there used to be. In fact on Durham's wild and wind-wracked western moors there used to be three no less!

You still don't believe me? Then listen to this story and I'll *prove* that it's true.

The three giants were brothers, of course. Their mother and father went in for big lads, but they skimped a bit on their names to make up for it. They called them Cor, Ben and Con. (Some folk say that the locals named three towns after them, that's Corbridge, Benfieldside and Consett.)

As they grew up they must have been a right worry to their parents. It's enough of a problem feeding one giant, but three! Can you imagine it?

'Mam! I'm hungry!'

'But you've just had that dead sheep for your breakfast!'

'Aw, Mam! I'm a growing lad.'

THE CONSETT GIANTS

'I was hoping you'd stopped growing by now. You're the only bairn in the village that can pinch the lead off the church roof while he's standing in the graveyard,' the mother moaned.

'I'll not do that again – I got caught,' Con complained.

'Why, lad, of course you got caught! You left a footprint on Maggie Mitson's grave ... and there's not many people in Durham takes a size seventy-three in boots!'

Con sighed. 'I had to get some money from somewhere. I was dying for a bag of chips and Dad wouldn't give me a farthing.'

'Surely you never expected to get money off your father, Con,' his mother mocked. 'He's tighter than the laces in my corset.'

Suddenly the house began to shake until the soot streamed down the chimney. 'That sounds like our brother Ben in a hurry,' Con said.

'Well, he's not getting any dinner, so he needn't think he is,' the boy's mother muttered as she scraped the sooty scum off the soup pot over the smoking cinders. 'I'd clip the soft wassock round his ears ... if I had a set of ladders big enough to reach his ears.'

'Mam!' bellowed Ben. His voice cracked two windows and blasted thatch halfway across the county. 'Mam! Me dad's had an accident!'

'Nothing trivial, I hope,' the sour-faced woman snapped.

'He's dead!' Ben boomed.

'Dead!' said his mother managing to smother a smile. 'Poor old bloke! Poor tight-fisted, mealy-mouthed, penny-pinching old b . . . bloke,' she sighed. 'How did it happen?'

'Well, it seems he met a miser down by the river Derwent. They had a bet as to who could hold his breath under water the longest.'

'And?'

'And they both drowned.'

'That'll teach him,' mother gloated grimly.

Ben went down on his hands and knees and looked through the door of the house. 'I'm hungry, Mam, got anything to eat?'

His mother glared at him. 'How can you think of food with your poor father lying dead at the bottom of the river? And anyway I can't go shopping because I haven't any money.'

'Where are we going to get money from, Mam?' Con asked.

'You three lads will have to go out and work for it,' Mam said firmly.

'Work!' Ben gasped. 'But I'm only thirteen. I'm still at school.'

'Don't be daft. You lads haven't been at

school since you grew too big to get in the door,' his mother reminded him.

'But we don't know how to work, Mam,' Con claimed.

'Then it's about time you learned. Otherwise there'll be no dinner. You can start by knocking a coffin together for your Dad, save a bit on the cost of the funeral.'

Just as Ben was pulling up an oak tree to make a coffin, the third brother, Cor, ran up the road. 'Here, Ben! Farmer Fulwell's just broken his plough – he's sent it for dad to fix at the forge,' Con cried,

'But Dad's dead,' Con sighed.

'I know, but I thought that if *we* could mend it for fat old Farmer Fulwell then he'd pay us.'

'And we could use the money to buy food!' Ben exclaimed.

The excited young giants rushed down the hillside and made the good folk of Durham think that an earthquake had hit their homes.

Cor showed his brothers the plough with the buckled blade.

'It's buckled,' Ben said.

'We can see that bird-brained Ben,' Cor sighed. 'What we want to know is how do we fix it?'

'Hit it with a hammer,' Con suggested.

'I'll fetch Dad's hammer from the forge,' Ben offered and he covered the half mile in a dozen strides. He returned moments later with a heavy hammer that he handled like a toy.

'Hold the plough, Cor and I'll hit it with a hammer,' Con said.

Cor held the plough. His brother swung the heavy hammer and hit him on the hand. Con's eyesight wasn't too good.

Cor sucked his sore thumb and moaned. 'Your feeble eyes will be the death of me.' And that was true.

Ben took the hammer from his brother and rested the plough on the road. He swung the hammer and hit the plough. The cloud of dust that rose choked the young giants, but the plough was still buckled.

Cor coughed and cried, 'You should have used the anvil – dad always used the anvil.'

'Sorry,' Ben shrugged. He ran back to the forge and returned with the anvil tucked under his arm. Suddenly he swung the anvil over his head and brought it crashing down. (This time the dust cloud blotted out the sun in Durham for two days.)

Cor shook his shaggy head. 'Bird-brain Ben,'

he muttered. 'You're supposed to put the anvil on the ground. You put the plough on the anvil. You hit the plough with the hammer.'

'Oh,' Ben said. 'Put the hammer on the ground. Put the anvil on the hammer. Hit the anvil with the plough.'

Con snorted. 'You're both daft. Why don't you just take the end of the plough and bend it straight?'

'What do you think we're trying to do? Clean our finger nails with it?'

'No-o. I mean like this,' Con replied. The giant picked up the plough and peered at the twisted tip. He took it between a fat finger and a fatter thumb and bent it straight again.

Straight as a magpie's tail!

'Cor!' said Cor. 'That's clever!'

'It was easy,' Ben boasted. He took the plough and ran to Fulwell Farm. After tapping timidly on the door, and knocking it flat on the floor, the fat farmer charged out like his best bull.

'What do you want, you big brat?' the man asked.

'I've fixed your plough, sir,' said Ben, polite as ever.

'Put it in the barn, you oversized lout,' the

farmer snapped, rude as ever. Then the man picked up his door and jammed it back in the frame.

Ben scratched his head then tapped on the door again. The fat farmer poked his head through a paint-peeling window. 'What now, you over-long loon?'

'I want paying, please, sir,' Ben said.

'Paying!' the farmer exploded. His face turned purple as he choked at the thought. 'Paying? Just for knocking a bit of iron straight? Why, anyone could do that.'

'Then why didn't you do it, sir?' the youngster asked.

The farmer's eyes were like two well-sucked black-bullets. He tried a new argument and his voice changed to a creaky whine. 'I'm a poor man. I can only afford three or two coppers ... one if you're lucky. I'll pay you next Christmas.'

The mean man moved to close the window but Ben put a finger in the gap and held it open. 'Sorry, sir, but my brothers and I will be starved by next Christmas. I'd like to be paid now if you please, sir. And the price is one guinea.'

The farmer gasped for air and the red rims round his eyes glowed. 'A-a-a guinea! I'm not paying a guinea, in fact I'm not paying a penny.'

THE CONSETT GIANTS

'Oh,' Dan shrugged. 'I'll just go and tell my brothers. Maybe they'll be a bit cross,' he said with a soft smile. 'Perhaps they'll blow the thatch off your house, that's if you're lucky.'

'A new thatch is a five guinea job,' fat Farmer Fulwell fumed. 'You call that lucky? What happens if I'm unlucky?'

'Oh, if you're unlucky, and you catch them in a really bad mood, they might just pull your arms off,' the giant juvenile grinned. 'And two new arms is more than a five guinea job, sir.'

The farmer's fierce eyes flickered fearfully. 'I'll give you ten shillings ... I mean five.'

Ben's hands shot forward and grasped the old man's wrists. 'One guinea, please, sir,' he said.

'Fifteen shillings ... I mean eight!' came the quick reply.

Ben began to pull the two wrists apart. The old man was wobbling over the windowsill and something began to crackle in his arms.

'Ah ... ohh ... oooh ... sixteen shillings!'
Crackle!
'Yahh! ... a pound-a pound-a pound!'
Crackle!
'Yeeeh! A guinea then ... oh let go ... a guinea! I agree!'

Ben smiled gently. 'Agreed, then.'

The farmer glared and rubbed his arms. 'A guinea,' he grumbled. 'That's the price of three fat lambs at market.'

'Fine!' Ben beamed. 'I'll just take the lambs instead, if you don't mind, sir.'

Ben stepped into Farmer Fulwell's field and scooped up three surprised sheep. With one tucked under each arm and one in his hands he headed home. That night the giant brothers settled to a hearty supper and made their plans.

Within a week they were the most marvellous blacksmiths that Durham had ever seen. Where other blacksmiths took an hour to shoe a horse the brothers took ten minutes.

Cor could pick up the biggest carthorse and cradle it in his arms like a kitten. Con could twist the iron bar round his finger in a horse-shoe shape then snip it off with his teeth. Ben would then take the shoe and push the nails in with a thick thumb.

And the price was always the same: a guinea, or three fat lambs.

So the giants grew richer and fatter and richer and taller, till they were too big to live in the village. They moved out into the hills and slept beneath the stars.

And when their huge hands grew too fat to hoop the horse-shoes they tore the iron-ore from

THE CONSETT GIANTS

the Derwent hills and carried it to the Consett mills. But when evening came and the sun set over the moors the cry was always the same. 'Mam! I'm hungry.'

For three fat sheep were no longer enough to feed their faces. The harder they worked the hungrier they felt and the hungrier they became the harder they had to work to make the money to pay for the food.

'What we need is a hammer so that we can do more work in less time,' said clever Cor.

'What we need,' said Con, 'is a *big* hammer.'

'But to be big enough for us,' Cor calculated, 'it would have to be high as a house and half the length of that field. Where would we find such a hammer?'

'Funny you should say that!' came a small, sly voice from around the boot-straps of the brothers. They looked down to see a strange man dressed in a top hat and a black tail coat. (They could not see that the hat hid his horns and the coat craftily concealed the fiend's forked tail!)

'Who are you?' Ben asked.

'A friend,' the fiend replied. 'And it just so happens that I know where you can find the hammer you need.'

'How much?' said Cor.

'Nothing!' the little devil grinned. 'Just sign this paper here.'

'We can't write,' the brothers said.

'Don't worry,' the devil smiled. 'A cross will do.'

'I haven't a pen and ink,' Ben said.

'Then sign in blood.'

'What does it say?' careful Con asked peering at the parched paper.

'It says that if *I* give you the hammer then *you* agree to let me take your souls when you die.'

Ben looked at the bottom of his boot; it held a hole bigger than a vicar's halo. 'Well, my sole's not worth much, it's a deal!'

The brothers signed the contract with blots of blood-stained thumb-prints and the little devil showed then where they could find the huge hammer. It was hidden beneath the black water of the quarry pond.

Of course the giants didn't read the small print on the contract, people never do. But before the little man left them he said with a chuckle,'There's one thing I ought to tell you. Don't drop the hammer.'

'Why not?' Con asked.

'Because if you do it will disappear and so will you. Your bodies will vanish into a vapour

THE CONSETT GIANTS

as thin as the East wind, while your souls will be swept straight to the steaming hearths of Hell!' he cackled.

'Here! You never told us that!' Cor claimed.

'It's in the contract,' the little man said patting the paper that was pouched safe in his pocket.

'But we can't read!' Con complained.

The devil shrugged and gave a sly smile. 'Shame,' he sniggered. And then he was gone as quick as Christmas.

'What will we do?' Cor cried.

'We'll make sure we don't drop the hammer, that's what we'll do,' Ben said.

So for many months they handled the huge hammer as carefully as a glass butterfly. They passed it gently from giant hand to giant hand. But as the months multiplied to make years the giants grew careless. The brothers moved from home to the hills around the Derwent and each grew too tired to go and fetch the hammer whenever he needed it.

Instead he would whistle.

Cor in Corbridge would throw it to Ben in Benfieldside or to Con in Consett and that's nine miles as the crow flies, or should I say as the hammer flew.

Nine miles may be a hard hike for little legs

like yours or mine, but it's just a few short steps for a giant.

It became a familiar scene in Western Durham.

Whistle!

'That'll be our Ben,' the boys' mother smiled as she rocked in her rich retirement chair.

Whoosh!

'There goes the hammer! Wait for it!'

Slaaap!

'Well caught, Con,' she sighed and smiled. For though the giants forgot the curse as the years drifted by on the tide of time, their mother never did.

And neither did the devil.

And the devil grew impatient.

So, maybe he was to blame for the accident.

It began when Con's clear eyes began to cloud. Evenings seemed to come more quickly to Con than they did to his brothers. And the flying hammer became blurred.

Whistle-whoosh-slaaap! became Whistle-whoosh-slip!

'Butter-fingers,' Ben yelled.

Con grinned as weakly as a candle in the mid-day sun. 'Just a joke,' he lied.

'Hah!' Ben grumbled. 'Your jokes will be the death of me!'

And Con shivered when he thought of what would happen if that hammer had hit the ground. So the next day Con took two or three steps closer to Cor, about a mile, before he whistled.

Whistle!

Cor threw the hammer.

Whoosh!

Cor aimed the hammer to land at Consett but Con had moved a mile nearer to his brother. The hammer almost flew over his head! At the last moment Con's weak eyes saw it. His hand shot up.

Slip-sliiip-slaaap!

That was close. Yet strangely Con felt a little better after that. The next day he took three steps towards Cor, and the day after four.

By the end of the week he was half way to Corbridge and still his luck held.

It wasn't until the ninth day that his luck changed.

Con took nine huge strides towards Corbridge.

Whistle!

At that moment a northern wind stung Con's eyes to tears. A flurry of snow, or maybe it was a handful of the devil's dust blinded him.

Whoosh!

He heard the hiss of the hammer and took one more desperate step towards his brother.

Even then he might have caught it. But the devil was desperate to collect his dues. Con's arm reached upwards but his foot caught on an old stone cottage. He stumbled. He gave a cry of horror as the hammer hurried over his head.

The giants' mother stopped her sewing. She waited for the sound of the catch. It never came. Perhaps she's waiting still.

Some say that the hammer landed at Howden; it gave the place the hollow dene and that's how Howden got its name. Perhaps that's true.

One thing is for certain. The giants disappeared.

Remember I said I'd *prove* this story true?

Well, you go to Benfieldside or Corbridge or Consett today. You won't see a single giant. They *must* have vanished, so the story must be true!

Of course to take the place of the three giant iron workers they had to build a giant iron works at Consett.

Today even those iron works have vanished in as sadly-strange a way as the three giants Cor, Ben and Con.

Someone must have dropped a hammer.

Some ideas for writing

* Write a tall story of your own designed to explain how a feature of the area you live in came to be. For example, you could explain why a river flows where it does; how your town got its name; why a street market happens where it does; how a hill was formed. If you do a bit of research in your local library or by talking to old neighbours you may be able to include some facts or local beliefs in your story.

* Rewrite this story as a play. You must keep the main characters the same although you could introduce a couple more characters. You could stick fairly closely to the dialogue in the story or make up new words for your characters. Remember to set out your play properly. (Look at a play in another book if you've forgotten how to do this.)

CLIFF

David Rees

David Rees was born in London and has recently returned to live in Hackney. In between he lived in Devon where he was a lecturer at the University of Exeter. He has written many novels and short stories for young people which have been published here and in America – a country he has visited several times.

David Rees's other Knockout is *Waves*.

Cliff

This is a very descriptive story about a person pushing himself to the limits. Although you may not have climbed a dangerous cliff you have probably been in a situation where you have been so frightened you think you cannot continue and yet you cannot turn back. The author has tried to describe through the events of this story exactly how that feels.

Cliff

Rain drumming on the tent roof woke me. It was so dark that not even the faintest outlines could be seen; only Paul's deep-sleep breathing just by me and those fairy drumsticks pattering on the canvas proved that anything still existed. I turned over. Tightness down in my bladder had woken me, but it was snug in the warm sleeping-bag; I was not going to get up. It was daft; why did it have to protest in the early hours? I unpeeled myself from the sleeping-bag, and groped for the flaps. After the tent's sleepy heat the cold of the ground shocked me into full consciousness; my feet squelched in the wet mud and the rain on my warm nakedness was like needles.

Back in the tent I curled up in a ball in the hot sleeping-bag: it was good to be zipped in, much more satisfying than being in a bed with sheets. Disturbed by my movements, Paul muttered in his sleep, and licked his lips several times.

In the morning I was first to wake, and I crept out, leaving Paul to snore. It had stopped raining, but the clouds were down low over the mountains, grey and smoky, not a break in them. The scree that scarred the nearby hillside glistened after the rain, the boulders at its foot wet and sharp, looking as if they had only rolled to rest a moment ago.

'Lousy weather,' said Paul, emerging.

'What are you going to do this morning?'

He looked at the clouds. 'Not climbing, anyway. We won't see the top at all.' He dabbed gingerly at the ground with one foot. 'Maybe right for a spot of fishing. Yes, I think I'll go fishing.' He looked towards the stream, still invisible in the mist, down among the grey jumble of rocks and pebbles.

'I think I'll take a walk down to the sea and try the cliff,' I said.

'What . . . climbing?'

'Why not?'

'Is it safe?'

I shrugged. 'I don't know. Seemed all right the other evening.'

'So you've had a look. I might have guessed. What about breakfast, eh? Bread and marmalade? It's too wet for a fire.' He went back to the tent. 'Tell you what,' he said, rummaging around in his pack for a knife, 'If you're not back in reasonable time, I'll come down after you and look for your bits and pieces.'

The stream gurgled and sucked along beside me, lapping round blocks of granite that its winter force had dragged down from the mountains. It was cold; the cliffs, I had reckoned, would be hot work, so I was wearing only shorts, sweater and sneakers.

The tide was coming in, slowly rubbing out the lines of rock. Bright ribbons of weed, amber and rust, and shell-fish in pools, limpets and winkles, softened the hard grey shapes of the beach. For the first time that day I noticed the birds– a solitary gannet, wings cutting the air like scissor blades, then a little colony of gulls, dazzling white feathers on a rock, patiently watching the incoming sea, and out beyond the waves, small diving birds, brown and in pairs, disappearing then bobbing up yards away, busy with activity. Shattered rocks marked the limit of this beach; they were knotty pointing fingers, threatening vengeance at the clouds, and lines of dogs' teeth suggesting a petrified monster beneath the sea. The cliff I was going to climb was the end of the hill that formed one side of the valley down which I had just walked. The vertical drop showed a cross-section of the hill's inside, an X-ray of its bones and nerves. The hill was a shoulder heaving up through the earth: it had been frozen in its upward thrust centuries ago in pre-history, and whatever earthquake or glacier had caused it had also torn half the limb away, and ripped it into thousands of fragments which were now the wilderness of boulders scattered about the beach at its base.

I started. The route, or at least half of it, had been worked out in my mind's eye the other evening when I came down for a swim. I was alone then as now – Paul had stayed by the fire to cook the fish he had caught – and I wondered if any other human had ever swum here. I had noticed on that occasion the diagonal fracture in the rock: it was a line, about two feet wide, that rose up about half-way, a hundred and fifty feet perhaps.

The fault did not rise as evenly as I had thought. In places it became almost level, making little platforms on which birds had nested earlier in the year. I paused on the third platform, looking down at the sea slowly rising over the rocks. When I started again, my feet slipped. My right leg cracked down hard on the ledge, and when the moment of terror was over, I found I was gripping a protruding turret of stone. I looked down through my legs, and there was only air between me and the spiked rocks on the beach.

I pulled myself upright. The fall had merely grazed the skin, but there were voices advising me to return to sea-level while there was still time. But I went on, up. As I heaved and kicked my way up the next vertical section, I looked only at my hands and arms and knees and the patches of cliff-face they were negotiating. My fingertips fumbled for the edge of stone that would hold. Then the biceps pulled: I heaved with my arms and dragged myself a few inches higher; with my knees jammed into a chink was safe. Up went a leg as high as it could stretch, so that the toe-cap of the plimsoll could feel the safety of the next cranny; another heave of the biceps, and I was lying on the next, almost flat, step. Little springs of perspiration trickled down into my eyes, and I was glad now I was wearing only sweater and shorts. I thought of arms dissected, as in a biology book diagram, and the labelled cross-section: muscle from humerus to scapula, biceps (flexes arm), triceps (extends arm), ulna, muscles which flex wrist and fingers, ligaments holding carpals. That was all it was, a system of levers, pulleys, hinges and joints for dragging and pulling. Yet the bicep, knotted into its tight ball, was one of the signs of strength, of being nearly a man, no longer the sleek and satin upper arm of a boy: some obscure urge always said that it must be better to be a man than a boy, and the stronger and more powerful the signs of a man the better. It was only because I wanted to prove I was less weedy than other people: it was stupid climbing up cliffs just to test such childishness. Nevertheless, it had to be done.

I stopped again. It was not so worrying now, looking at the sea. The rocks down there had merged into their surroundings; they were not half so fierce as close to. I dangled my legs over the edge, and deliberately looked down, humming a tune. 'Do not forsake me, oh my darling ... on this our wedding day.' The pools the tide had not yet reached were mirrors without reflections; the breeze ruffled their surfaces, spoiling the upturned clouds I could see there. The white edges of waves fretted the rocks, and occasionally sent up a column of spray. The sound was gentle and soothing, a wordless dirge for several voices. Above, the clouds still drifted. On my own level were the birds. A black-backed gull flew by, very near, its wings making a flap-flap-flap noise like a book being shut several times in succession. There were other birds I did not recognize, petrels and skuas maybe, and once I saw a puffin, perched on a stone much higher up, solemn and judge-like. I continued the journey, arms, legs and sweater now filthy from the rock. At last I was on the wide shelf one hundred and fifty feet up, where the diagonal flaw ended.

Here was the surprise of the climb: a cave. It extended back no more than a few feet, and it was not high enough for me to stand upright. It was not much more than a hole. I sat down, cross-legged, in the entrance and peered at the walls; they were just slightly redder than the rest of the grey stone, as was the dust on the floor. A person could live here. I could bring up food in a pack and hide for weeks. It wasn't impossible; people had lived in worse places. But there was no sign of anyone having tried it. There were bird remains all over the ledge outside, just like further down. It seemed to be a favourite nesting site, for there were not only feathers, but bits of twig, some skeletons of small unidentifiable creatures, and white and yellow stains all across the stone.

The sea breaking on the rocks below was out of sight under the overhang, so its sound, too, was cut off: instead of the restless falling and gathering of white waves, there was this grey-blue sheet stretching out below, heaving and wrinkling; I could almost hurl myself down there, I thought, and its embrace would be like soft blue wool. I looked up to avoid the growing insistent pull of the drop, and wondered if it was possible to climb any higher. There was no immediately obvious route. The cliff rose sheer, though there were buttresses and pinnacles of rock to cling to in places. I thought again of the mighty crash that had caused it all. Had one half of the hill really been ripped away? I imagined the noise, the segments of stone splitting off, the landslide of earth, the terror of prehistoric beasts caught near it.

The cave, this central point of the cliff to which the path had led, might have been the home of some prehistoric person, who could skip with ease up the crack I had just laboriously climbed. I took off my sweater. It was wrong here, with this landscape, sea and sky, to wear such a civilized thing. I pressed my arm against the stone. Despite its rough texture and durability, I would shin up the rest of it regardless of any power it had to hurt. I would almost welcome the fight with it, the rock trying to scratch and tear at me.

I lay on my front and leaned over the edge. The tide had sunk all the beach and was beginning its daily battering of the cliff-foot. Life would have ceased before it could scour out passages into this rock big enough to cause another fall. The white water drained back under the succeeding wave and as that, in turn, crashed against the cliff, spray surged up, then fell back on the surface, slap-slap-slap. Again it happened. Again. Again, again, again.

It was a long way down. I imagined myself falling. It would be certain death down there. I'm too young to die. Sixteen years and four months. At that age, they say, you have your whole life before you. The slow painful growing was nearly over; the body-machine would soon be developed to its peak, and the mind was stuffed, or almost stuffed, with the required knowledge and certificates. I had just finished my GCSEs. Besides, the death down there would mean pain; there would be no gentle slipping into the white lace of the waves; or, as I had imagined earlier, sinking in blue wool. Drowning, suffocation in water: I remembered fish on a river bank, their violent, uncontrollable spasms as they asphyxiated in air. Worse would be the rocks, shattering bones out of their pattern of joints, or the smash of light as the face met stone, or being impaled, the pinnacle ripping up through me.

I pushed back from the edge and stood up.

These things were not going to happen; they were only fantasies, and like so many fantasies about death or violence done to me, they ended with worries about remaining alive, maimed or paralysed for life. How was I to climb higher? The rocky face stretched up, but the ledge I was standing on was not wide enough for me to be able to see the top of the cliff. A bird hovered in the sky, a buzzard perhaps, and above it, the clouds still moved majestically inland. My sweater. I put it on; it was clammy with cool sweat.

There were three or four obvious holds to begin with; in a matter of minutes I was high above the ledge and the cave disappeared from view. Then trouble started. I was right up under an overhang, and the sensible course was to return to the ledge. Suddenly I was afraid. Going down, now that I thought of it, presented all sorts of difficulties. I would have to keep both hands and one foot firmly in the slits the cliff afforded while the other foot stretched out, stubbing for a fissure lower down. Suppose it did not find it? Or if it found the wrong one, how could I tell whether it was safe or not? I imagined the loose rock crumbling, the feet sliding out into space; the arms, caught by surprise, unable to sustain this sudden lurch of the body: and I would be hurtling through air. For a moment or two I was frozen with fear, and I crouched up under the overhang, too terrified to look at the sea. I would not go down, I decided, under any circumstances, even if it meant the indignity of waiting for Paul and a rescue party.

Perhaps I could edge myself sideways? There was a handhold to the left, and a tussock of grass. Grass was normally not to be trusted at all, but this time it would have to be; there were no footholds, for the face was smooth, almost polished. I put my left hand round the grass and tugged. It seemed safe, but it would have to share my whole weight with the rim over which I curved my right hand; and it would have to hold while I hauled myself up. If it broke, nothing would stop me from plunging onto the rocks. My mother's face came into my mind. The grass held; for a second as I trusted myself to it completely I looked down and saw my bare legs dangling in air, and miles below, the sea.

I was safe, but still scared. By now I could have been dead. How crazy it was to have come on my own! I had no food, and if it was impossible to climb any further I might starve to death. If I had to stay here for any length of time, my clothes were quite unsuitable, and if I was rescued, there would be all the disturbance of the lives of other people who had to come out to look for me, the lectures and moralisings, the uncomfortable inferiority to wise old Paul, the sense of failure and shame in myself. There was one cheering thought, however: the patches of grass meant I could not now be far from the top.

The going was a little easier, and I scrambled up a gully between tall crags. There were deep rifts in these, so that at times what I thought was part of the cliff turned out to be a stack, a gigantic slab, only attached to the main rock structure at its base, and it soared up, separate. Some of the crevices were wide enough to climb into; one of them might provide an easy route to the top. At the head of the gully the wall was sheer and smooth, so I squeezed sideways into the nearest of these miniature chasms. It was the bleakest, most desolate part of the journey. Behind and in front were walls of rock, black and damp, and it was so quiet that my breathing roared. The ascent now required considerable physical effort. I kept both feet pressed against the wall in front, and my hands and arms on the wall behind. Very slowly I levered myself up. The boy sweeps in Victorian times must have clambered up chimneys in this way. Eventually my head popped out like the sweep's broom, and I could see at once how vast the sky really was and how far off was the sea.

I was bleeding. I had cut both wrists in crawling up that dark slot. There were tears in my shorts, one six inches long up the side. One more push; I was out of the darkness of the chasm, and panting on the clayey soil. I'd done it! There was grass, heather in bloom, and little black rabbit droppings. I could not get used, for the first few steps, to the notion that I did not have to worry about where I was going to put my feet. I leaned over for a last look, and thought, I beat you; I'm one you didn't get.

Paul had a fire going. For a moment it was all foreign, another human being going about his peaceful pursuits; my eyes were still full of ancient rock-faces and vast panoramas.

'Want some fish?' he asked.

The smell brought me back to the world — chips, wet Friday nights, suburbs. I was hungry.

'Please.'

'You're filthy.'

'It's a rough old climb.' I looked at the fish bubbling in the pan. He had even managed to put breadcrumbs on them.

'They won't be ready for a while; I've just put

them on. There's some spuds in the bottom of the fire, too.'

'I'm going to have a bath.'

I took off my clothes and threw them into the tent, then picked up a towel and walked down to the stream. I was tired now, and my arms and legs were beginning to ache. I was looking forward to the time after the wash when I would be warm and dry and full of hot food, and a sleepy contented relaxation would come as I finished a bottle of beer.

We had discovered the deep pool in the stream on the first day. The icy rushing water was always a stab of pain at first, but it would soon ease. I stepped in, and propping my arms round two convenient stones let the stream pour over my shoulders. My body dangled down in the pool and the speed of the water kept me half-afloat. When I had recovered my breath and the cold sensation had lessened so I could relax a little, I began to enjoy it. My body was rising and falling in the current. I ducked my head under, and opened my eyes: grey, flying movement of water. There could be no drowning in this. I came up, gasping, and shook my hair.

'Dinner is served,' said Paul.

The clouds were lifting; the crags on the

Scoir were visible. Tomorrow we would go up there. It was the highest mountain.

'We've run out of beer,' Paul said.

'We'll have to walk to Shawbost, then.'

'It's five miles.'

'What's five miles?' I scrambled out and started to dry myself. 'I should be worn out, but I could walk twenty.'

He laughed. 'Come and eat the fish.'

As I ate the fish, burning my fingers on it (I never used knives and forks on this sort of trip) I realised the fire was making me drowsy.

'It's a funny thought,' said Paul, a few moments later. 'This time last week you were tired, but that was because you'd spent the previous evening at a disco. Now look at you.'

But I heard little of this; I was nearly asleep, and my dream was forcing me up the cliff again. This time the grass gave way, and I fell, clutching it in my hand. I woke, gasping.

The last cloud lifted from the Scoir, and the sun came out for the first time that day.

Some ideas for writing

* Go through the story listing words and phrases that catch your attention as the climb, the moment of panic and the escape are described. Next, using some of these words and phrases together with ones you make up, write a poem called *Cliff* which describes a similar experience to the one in the story. If you find a poem too difficult write a description instead.

* Either remember or invent a time when you were in a similar situation where you felt scared, powerless and unable to go forwards or back. This could be swimming out of your depth; being involved in an accident; standing up for yourself against an authority figure; being prepared for an operation; or a visit to the dentist! Describe your feelings as the situation develops as clearly as you can using David Rees's story as a model.

The Typewriter...

Beverley Naidoo

Beverley Naidoo lived in South Africa until she was twenty-two when she came to England to study at the University of York. She has taught in primary and secondary schools in London. Beverley Naidoo now lives in Bournemouth with her husband and two children.

Beverley Naidoo's first work of fiction for young people was a Knockout *Journey to Jo'burg* which has already won two prizes, the Other Award in Britain and the Child Study Association Award in America.

The Typewriter

This story gives some idea of what it must have been like to be a school student in Soweto in the late 1970s. It is probably quite difficult for you to understand that Nandi's experiences in this story, as she helps her older cousin Esther resist the forces of oppression, are experiences shared by thousands of young black people in South Africa today. Using a real situation and the kinds of experiences common to many people the author has constructed a story rich in suspense which is also designed to leave the reader thinking about world events.

The Typewriter

To the children of Soweto, 1976
To those who went before and
to those who have followed.

'Here, read this! Give it to your parents!'
Someone thrust a leaflet into Nandi's hand. She glanced at it, keeping in step with the steady march of school students on their way to the cemetery.

> *PARENT-WORKERS! DO NOT GO TO WORK ON MONDAY! We the black students of South Africa have left our schools to fight the oppressors who keep us down. We want to write exams, but not while the police are murdering our brothers and sisters.*
>
> *Parents, you should be proud to have children who prefer to die from bullets than swallow the poison in our schools.*
>
> *Parent-workers, hear our call and STAY*

AWAY FROM WORK ON MONDAY! We have nothing to lose but our chains!

For the last few weeks Nandi's school had been closed. From the news on Radio South Africa it seemed that all over the country black students were refusing to go to classes. Some schools had even been burnt down. Everywhere the cry was rising, 'Down with Bantu Education!' 'Down with White Rule!'

With news of shootings and mass arrests, Nandi's mother worried constantly about leaving her children when she was out at work in the factory. Nandi was eleven and the twins barely three years old. But Ma had no choice, except to ask old Ma Tabane, their neighbour, to keep an eye on them.

Ma had been especially anxious about today. It was to be the funeral of two students from the high school, shot by police a week ago. Before leaving for work early that morning, Ma had told Nandi very firmly, 'Don't go out at all. There'll be trouble for sure.'

Nandi hadn't wanted to disobey Ma, but when she had heard the shouts and the singing so close to the house, she had felt unable to resist. Her little brother and sister had been playing happily in the back yard. Ma Tabane

THE TYPEWRITER

had been hanging out washing next door, calling over to them occasionally. She was rather deaf and her crackly old radio blared out music which seemed to cover the other sounds being carried in the air. Quietly Nandi had slipped out through the front of their small box house and into the dry stony street. With luck no one would notice she was missing for a short while.

Marching along with hundreds of students, dust rising from under their feet, Nandi now carefully folded the leaflet she had been told to give to her mother, putting it in her pocket. She wasn't sure what Ma would say about it. There was also the problem that if she gave it herself, Ma would know her order had been disobeyed. She would have to ask Esther to pass it on. Her cousin was sixteen. Living with Khulu, their granny, Esther seemed free to do so many things Ma would never let Nandi do. When Khulu went off to work each day to sell fruit in Johannesburg, Esther also didn't have to stay at home looking after younger children.

Nandi kept looking for Esther in the crowd. It was certain she was there, probably near the front. The older students usually led the way, carrying home-made banners and hurling their voices into the air. Nandi knew all the freedom songs by now. Esther and her friends had taught them to her. But this was electric, so many people singing together what they felt.

'We are the young people,
We will not be broken!
Come with your cannons,
Come with your guns!
We demand freedom
and say
"Away with slavery
In our land of Africa!"'

Nandi's voice mingled with the rest. At least their voices were free. Street after street, past rows of box houses all like her own, hundreds of feet and voices stirred up those who were not working in the city. Faces appeared at doors and windows. Little children ran out shouting before being pulled back by firm elderly hands. A voice from the side rang out,

'Go back home! You youngsters are asking for trouble!'

'Don't worry, Baba[1]! We're ready for it!' someone shouted back.

Another old man, struggling off a chair in his front yard, raised up an arm and fist.

'Amandla[2]!' he called in a wavery, thin voice.

'Ngawethu[3]!' thundered students passing by, cheering and waving to him.

As students neared the cemetery however, the mood suddenly changed. A halt in the march brought students packing in on each other. Up ahead, beyond the banners, Nandi could see that the cemetery gates were closed; barred around by rows of police and gigantic grey tanks, like steel monsters with great square black eyes. A voice was barking through a loudspeaker: 'YOU ARE TO GO HOME IMMEDIATELY! ONLY FAMILIES OF THE DECEASED MAY ENTER!'

The crowd roared back: 'THEY WERE OUR BROTHERS! LET US IN!'

Suddenly a great cry rose up. Choking, coughing, eyes stinging, blinded with something fierce and burning, Nandi found herself being pushed and pulled to avoid the swinging, crashing batons. Stones skimmed over-head towards the police as the school children began to push back desperately, scattering to find cover, fearing more of the terrifying gun-shots. The same gun-shots that brought them to the cemetery today to sing their songs for the two already dead. Once again, songs had turned to screams and cries. Nandi could hear her own

[1] Father
[2] Power
[3] To the people

voice ringing out as she ran home. Above it echoed sharp, fearful cracks through the air.

No-one saw Nandi slip back into the house. She grabbed her rope and began to skip vigorously out in the front to cover up her shaking. When Ma Tabane came to sweep the dirt out of her front door, she shook her head slightly.

'Ai, Nandi! You'll finish yourself like that!'

Ma came home later than usual. There had been a rush job at the factory and she had been ordered to work over-time. She knew already there had been trouble at the cemetery.

'You stayed at home?'

Nandi nodded.

'Did Esther come here today?'

'No Ma.'

'Tch! That boss has no heart!'

Ma spoke angrily. She looked upon her brother's child as her own and wouldn't be at ease until she knew Esther was safe. But now, with the curfew, it was too late for a half-hour walk through the dark streets of Soweto to Khulu's house. Nandi kept very quiet, trying not to let the pictures in her mind show on her face.

Tap-tap. Tap-tap-tap.

At first it seemed part of her dream that night . . .

THE TYPEWRITER

Nandi was acting 'look-out' for Esther and her friends as they held a secret meeting in the tiny, cramped kitchen while Khulu and the neighbours were all out at work. Nandi's job was to play outside, but if she saw anyone strange enter the road she had to warn Esther immediately so the others could slip away through the back. She was pretending to be busy skipping in and out through the gate, when she heard the tapping. It sounded as if the students were typing. Then Nandi realised the rhythm was wrong. She froze. Whatever was it? She wanted to call out a warning signal, but somehow her open mouth had become stiff . . .

Nandi woke up, feeling panic. The tapping was real, coming softly from the window. Then everything was silent for a few seconds, except for the breathing of the twins sleeping next to her. It was very dark, probably after mid-night. No noises came from outside now – no running footsteps, no odd shouts or cries, no roaring of police vans.

Nandi gripped her breath and waited.

Tap-tap-tap-tap-tap.

The soft tapping came more rapidly. Her heart drummed as she forced herself from the bed to the window.

'Who is it?' she whispered.

'It's me ... Esther! Open quickly!'

Carefully, she released the latch and leaned forward. The shape of her cousin was pressed up against the wall. Before Nandi could say anything, Esther began:

'Look Nandi, I need help!'

'Ah! Are you hurt?'

Esther was shaking, clutching her arm. Her voice was low and hoarse.

'It's nothing ... later ... there's something urgent!'

Breathing heavily, the older girl explained. In the afternoon she and her friends had been close to the cemetery gates. Themba and Zinzi had been carrying a banner saying: 'THEY DIED FOR FREEDOM'.

When the police attacked, both Themba and Zinzi had been grabbed. Esther had escaped, although a baton had whipped down on her arm. She had seen both her friends being beaten about their heads and thrown like sacks into a police van.

Esther feared the worst. Everyone knew the police stopped at nothing to get information. There were funerals to prove it. So it wouldn't be long before they would be coming for her too. Even now, someone could be secretly watching Khulu's house, waiting ... But worse, they might have started searching the house – and then Khulu would be in terrible trouble.

'It's the typewriter, Nandi. For our leaflets. I hid it – but if they find it, they'll arrest Khulu. They won't believe she knows nothing!'

Nandi sucked in her breath, horrified. Esther continued.

'It's not only Khulu. That typewriter can send us to jail for a long time.'

'Can't we do something? Can't I get a message to Khulu?'

'It's dangerous. Not a game.'

'I know ... but I can try ... first thing in the morning. If someone is watching the house, I can look as if I'm going to help Khulu.'

Esther said quietly,

'It's very risky ... but it's our only chance. There's no one else I can ask.'

'Where is the hiding place?' asked Nandi simply.

Briefly Esther explained that the typewriter was hidden behind the kitchen cupboard, wrapped in brown paper. Nandi and Khulu would have to pull away the panel at the back. To get rid of the package, she said they should stuff it in the dustbin outside the back-door and cover it well with the rubbish. If the police didn't find it in their search, it might even be possible for a friend to retrieve it later.

'But what if the back of the house is being watched?'

'Then we're trapped,' replied Esther.

Although her voice was steady, her cousin was still clutching her arm.

'Where will you go? What about your arm?'

'I'll find somewhere ... and tell Khulu I'm sorry ...' Esther paused.

'It had to be done. Tell her not to worry. I'll send her a message as soon as I can.'

Nandi's eyes followed Esther's bent shape making its way across the yard. After closing the window, trying not to let it squeak, she crept back into bed to wait for the morning. She curled herself up small and tight, as if to hold in her fear and stop it from growing.

It was impossible to take her mind off Esther stumbling away into the dark to look for a 'safe' house ... Themba and Zinzi being hit about the head ... Themba who always greeted Nandi with a wink and his 'How's it sis?' ... Zinzi with her warm smile and special way of swinging your hand in friendship. Both looked on her as a younger sister. When she had acted as 'look-out' for their meetings, she had known it was something serious, yet it had still been a bit like a game. Although she had known there was danger, it was also exciting. But what she had to do this time contained no enjoyment, no excitement of that kind at all. The danger was all around now. When she began to think of Khulu, her mind blocked off. The police couldn't harm her. No, no . . .

Nandi set off at first light, slipping out before her mother was up. She left a note: Gone to Khulu.

Nandi wasn't sure what to tell Ma when she returned. It was too difficult to sort out at the moment. Later, after taking the message, she would think about it.

Grey mist hung over the streets and the early morning air was chilly. Nandi hugged her arms around her as she ran. Already a stream of people were walking steadily towards the station. In the half light they seemed almost like ghosts, pulled by some invisible cord towards the city. Their grandmother usually set off for work early herself, so Nandi had to hurry. Perhaps Khulu had gone out looking for Esther. She must be so worried . . . and how would she be on hearing the message . . . angry, upset, frightened? Nandi refused to let herself imagine the police in the house itself.

Along the way Nandi could see the signs of people's fury. The place where Ma came to pay the rent was a heap of smouldering rubble, smoke mingling with the mist. Further on, the roof of the high school was missing, the walls blackened and windows shattered. She ran on, pausing only at one point to press herself against a fence as a police patrol truck thundered past.

Near Khulu's road, out of breath and panting, Nandi stopped to lean against a wall. If the police had set someone to watch the house, her arrival must seem absolutely normal. It was impossible to prevent her heart from throbbing, but once her breathing had slowed down a little, she walked on.

Turning the corner, she saw the strange car immediately. It was parked a little way up the road from the house, with its bonnet raised and two men bending over the engine. One was holding a torch. Perhaps they were genuine and had really broken down. But why so close to Khulu's? How could you know if they were informers? She had heard Esther and her friends discussing walkie-talkies once. What if the torch was one? Nandi had to walk right past, quite casually. Close to the car, she found herself humming the tune of one of the students' songs very softly to herself. It seemed to give her courage. The man with the torch glanced directly up at her as she passed. Reaching Khulu's front yard at last, she clicked the gate carefully behind her. With the feeling that eyes were following her, she made her way around to the back door, out of sight.

From the moment she had come home the evening before, after her day in Johannesburg, Khulu had known something was wrong. News had begun spreading earlier in the day among the flat workers near where Khulu sold fruit. A mid-afternoon radio report had mentioned 'trouble at a funeral'. Later, bill-boards for the evening newspaper had been headlined FUNERAL SHOOTING: THREE DEAD.

By the time Sowetans were making their long journey home by train, some had read the first reports. Their comments had weaved rapidly through the tightly crowded carriages. Parents and grandparents had made silent prayers.

Outside the station Khulu had found heavily armed police, moving people on; ordering them to go straight home and stay inside. A great tank had come roaring down the road and up the hill. Smoke and flames had been rising from the direction of the Rent Offices. Balancing her half-filled box of fruit on her head, Khulu had forced her tired body to move as quickly as it could. When finally she had found the house empty – and no food prepared – anxiety already burning within her had leapt up like a flame. It was true that sometimes Esther came in late, but there would always be some supper waiting in the pot, prepared by Esther earlier on.

Khulu had wanted to go out looking for her grandchild straight away. Was she one of those shot? Had she been hurt, or arrested? She would have to find one of Esther's friends. Yet what if something had happened to them too? Maybe in the end she would have to ask at the police station. She had just been starting up the road again, when her neighbour's husband had called out to her. Hadn't she heard the police message? They were going to shoot anyone on the streets at night. Khulu had halted. She could hear the rumble of tanks; could see smoke rising in different places; could smell burning in the air. She was not young any more and could not have moved quickly to take cover like the youngsters on the street corners. Wearily she had returned to the empty house, to wait till the morning.

THE TYPEWRITER

All night Khulu had sat up. When the knocking came early in the morning, she hurried to the door. Could it be Esther at last? Instead, there was Nandi, almost falling onto her and stammering her message.

What happened next was something that remained for a long time in Nandi's mind like a silent film. Without saying a word, her deeply lined face very grave, Khulu lowered herself with difficulty onto her knees beside the cupboard. Her worn, wrinkled hands passed Nandi two old grey saucepans and a bent frying pan, before the two of them loosened and lifted out the back panel. It was there. Together they pulled out the heavy brown paper parcel.

'What rubbish can we throw on top?' Nandi whispered.

Khulu signalled for Nandi to wait. She heaved herself up. Then taking the box in which she carried fruit to sell, she tipped out apples, oranges and bananas onto the bed. Lifting the brown paper package, she placed it at the bottom of the box and began to pile the fruit on top of it. It was all done in a couple of minutes. There was another small box of fruit on a chair. She pointed to it.

'Bring that!' she said to Nandi.

Nandi was speechless. Whatever was Khulu going to do with the typewriter?

Slowly Khulu raised the large box onto her head, balancing it carefully. Nandi did the same with the small one and followed her grandmother out of the back door. Khulu led the way across the small yard to a narrow gap in the back fence. There was a point in crossing the yard where the men by the car could see them if looking in that direction. But there was no sound of footsteps as they reached the back fence. Making their way silently between the opposite houses, they passed out into the next street.

Nandi desperately wanted to ask Khulu what she intended to do, but when she began to speak, Khulu shook her head. So, without knowing where they were going, Nandi followed her grandmother as they walked steadily onwards, the boxes swaying gently on their heads.

There were a couple of black policemen standing at the entrance to the station. Nandi's heart jumped as one of them put out a hand and lifted a bunch of bananas out of her grandmother's box.

'Thanks, Granny!', he said, tearing off a banana and throwing it to his mate. He didn't offer to pay, but Khulu simply turned to look at him, her grave face giving a slight nod.

THE TYPEWRITER

Khulu took her usual route to work: the overcrowded train into Johannesburg, then the overcrowded bus to the 'white' suburb with the tall blocks of flats. For the last thirty years she had come six days a week to sell fruit to people hurrying to or from cooking, cleaning and serving inside the homes of 'masters' and 'madams.'

Nandi had come with Khulu before, standing all day from early in the morning until late in the evening, at the corner of a big block of flats near the bus-stop. She had seen white people driving off in smart cars, long after Khulu and the other workers had arrived in the morning. She had seen the same white people driving back home, long before Khulu and the other black people set off on their tiring journey home to Soweto.

Nandi had seen white children in expensive uniforms, complete with hats and caps, walking or being driven to school; and coming home in the middle of the afternoon, licking ice-creams, laughing. The white children's school couldn't be like her own – of that she was sure, even though she hadn't seen it. In her school there were so many children that her class finished at eleven o'clock so that another lot of children could come in!

This morning as she stood at the same corner, Nandi's mind was in a turmoil. Whenever

Esther had spoken about what was so bad in their country, Khulu had usually remained quiet, getting on with her work. Only once Nandi could remember how she had put down her iron and said: 'You children always want things to happen so quickly! You think you are the first to fight ... and that it's easy!'

'But Khulu ...' Esther had begun.

'No, it's no use telling me ... I'm too old!' Their grandmother had shaken her head and started ironing again.

That was why this was so puzzling, startling ... Khulu acting so swiftly and calmly ... bringing the typewriter right into the middle of the 'white' suburb, almost under the noses of the police. Nandi wanted to ask why Khulu was doing this dangerous thing. Wouldn't it have been so much easier to throw the parcel away into the dustbin? Each time someone bought an orange, an apple or a banana, the layer of fruit got less. What did Khulu intend to do now?

Nandi waited for most of the passers-by to go into work and the street to quieten down before she whispered her question.

'Khulu, what are you going to do with it?'

Looking at the young worried face, Khulu smiled a little.

THE TYPEWRITER

'There's a place where it will be safe for a while ...' She paused, then added softly, 'How can I throw it away when the children still need it?'

Nandi moved up close to Khulu, resting against her, not saying anything more. Words were too difficult.

A little later, when the traffic of passing cars had lessened, Khulu left Nandi standing at the corner with the small box of fruit. Having placed the large box once again on her head, she slowly made her way up the street towards the drive-in entrance to the nearest block of flats. The security gate was open and all seemed quiet in the entrance which led to a court-yard with a row of open garages. Biting her lip, Nandi watched as Khulu walked through the entrance and then stopped by the first vacant garage. At the back of the garage Nandi could see a shelf cluttered with old cardboard boxes and junk. With a brief glance around her, Khulu walked inside. After putting the fruit box down on the floor, she lifted out the brown paper parcel.

At that moment a silver car came swerving around the corner where Nandi stood, turned into the driveway and directed itself towards the very garage where Khulu was wedging the package onto the shelf. A white woman with long red hair and high-heels stepped out of the car, screaming in English: 'What do you think you're doing? Come in here to steal, have you?'

Khulu shook her head, but didn't reply.

The screech continued. 'What's that you've been meddling with then? Let me see!'

Nandi ran towards the entrance, but stopped short as the white woman strode into the garage, pulled down the parcel onto the garage floor and ripped open the paper. There lay the typewriter, next to the box of oranges, apples and bananas.

'This isn't mine! It's stolen, isn't it! So you've come to hide it in my garage! Well you've been caught my girl!'

By now a small crowd of people had gathered near the garage. A large white man made his way through to the screaming woman. Khulu stood still, saying nothing.

'What's the trouble, Mrs Laker?'

'It's this thief here ...'

At the word 'thief,' Nandi forgot her own terror and ran to Khulu. She sobbed against her.

'You're not a "thief," Khulu! You didn't steal anything! Tell them! Please tell them!'

Khulu's body heaved as she held her granddaughter tightly for a few seconds. Then, from under her shawl, she slipped her little purse

THE TYPEWRITER

with its few coins into Nandi's pocket, saying very quietly,

'You must go home. The police mustn't find you here. Go right away ... and tell your mama not to worry. You MUST go!'

Nandi felt Khulu push her gently, but firmly, away, Nandi wanted to resist, to stay, but Khulu's face had such a still, sure look that reluctantly she began to move. The white woman was still going on in her high-pitched voice.

'The police won't be long now!'

Themba ... Zinzi ... now Khulu! Angry tears blurred out everything as Nandi edged through the small crowd and ran down to the corner, to collect the remaining box of fruit.

Travelling back alone on the train, Nandi thought about Ma. She wondered what Ma had made of her note and whether she had still gone to work. She didn't want to hurt Ma, but Nandi suddenly realised it was no longer a problem what to say, or how to cover up. The typewriter and everything else was now in the open. Searching in her pocket, she pulled out the leaflet from the march; the one she had wanted Esther to hand to Ma. Nandi re-read it.

'Parents you should be proud to have children who prefer to die from bullets ...'

The police had taken her friends, and now

her granny. Her cousin Esther may have escaped, perhaps to carry on fighting ... Well, she was proud of them! She would tell Ma all about it and give her the leaflet herself.

Eight months later there was a small item in a national newspaper:

GRANDMOTHER SENT TO JAIL

A 68-year old grandmother was sent to jail today for twelve months, after refusing to give evidence against two young students charged with sedition and terrorism.

The prosecution said that further charges might still be laid against Mrs Miriam Mabale for being in possession of a typewriter alleged to have been used by the accused in the preparation of leaflets calling for the boycott of 'apartheid schools', strikes and armed resistance.

The two accused, Themba Moya and Zinzi Dipale are alleged to be friends of Mrs Mabale's granddaughter Esther Mabale who is still being sought by the police.

Some ideas for writing

* Imagine you are a reporter sent to interview Khulu after she has served a prison sentence. Write what the grandmother has to say about the events leading up to her arrest and the continuing involvement and resistance of her grand-daughters Nandi and Esther. Her views about events in South Africa would be obvious in everything she said.

* Write a letter to Nandi or Esther expressing your own opinions about what you know about events in South Africa. Don't worry if you feel you don't know much. Use the events described in the story as well as what you have learnt from news programmes and newspaper reports. Your letter may contain warnings; may compare their situations with your own and may offer support.

Knockouts
Series editor: Jane Joyner
Founder editor: Josie Levine

The Girls and Yanga Marshall   James Berry
Plays for Today   Michael Church and Betty Tadman
Lesley's Life   Lesley Davies
Spine Chilling Stories   Terry Deary and Alan McLean
Walking Shadows   Terry Deary
I met her on a rainy day   Terry Deary
Don't dig up your granny when she's dead   Terry Deary
The Treasure of Skull Island   Terry Deary
The Ice House of Nightmare Avenue   Terry Deary
Love Stories   Harry Gilbert
Double Happiness   Pamela Grant
Hooked!   Michael Hardcastle
The Lord God made them all   James Herriot
* *A Northern Childhood: The Balaclava Story and other stories*
   George Layton
* *A Northern Childhood: The Fib and other stories*   George Layton
Time Rope   Robert Leeson
Time Rope: Three against the World   Robert Leeson
Time Rope: At war with tomorrow   Robert Leeson
Time Rope: The Metro Gangs Attack   Robert Leeson
A Taste of Freedom   Julius Lester
At the sign of the Dog and Rocket   Jan Mark
It's only rock 'n' roll   Alan McLean
The Ghost of the Glen   Alan McLean
Will of Iron   Gerard Melia
Silvertown Disaster   Gerard Melia
* *Journey to Jo'burg*   Beverley Naidoo
Waves   David Rees
* *The Bakerloo Flea*   Michael Rosen
Pickled Onions   Chris Shepherd
* *The trouble with Lindy's liftshaft*   Andy Smith
The Midwich Cuckoos   John Wyndham
Introductory Pack
Knockout Short Stories   Eight stories
Knockout Poems collected by John Foster

* Cassette available